A Job Seeker's Guide
Timeless Principles in Difficult Times

J. KEVIN HAND

Revised & Updated by Lauren Cabral

ACKNOWLEDGEMENTS

Celebrating the 25th year of Hand & Associates, Inc. has been a business milestone. This silver anniversary is longer than most marriages in the United States! All kidding aside, the years have passed quickly, risking it all on 28 credit cards so I could pay for the employees and all the expenses that were incurred. My thanks to all who have helped me and the employees of Hand & Associates over the quarter of a century. The idea that anyone would have told me that we would have done this; I would have called them insane. A special thanks to all the coaches, consultants, employees, customers and clients who have been a part of our success. Most importantly, this journey would not have happened if not for all of the people who have worked with me in the 25 years. The risks were high but the rewards were great. Much like this book, change is always there and one must embrace it so one can persevere in the end. This book is a gift from my team to you! This life is an adventure so embrace it! Opportunity is always there. Live joyfully and smile a lot at what life throws at you and you will conquer.

J. Kevin Hand
President/CEO
Hand & Associates

TABLE OF CONTENTS

INTRODUCTION

Finding a job in the 21st century has changed substantially. We have new tools as well as new challenges. Advancements in technology and constantly shifting global economies are key factors that have led to the daunting endeavor of today's job search.

The economy is a kind of living organism that constantly changes. The explosion of knowledge, the spread of information, the surge of technological innovation are continuing apace. Some markets are growing. Others are shrinking. Whole industries are shriveling up, while others are being spawned and transforming.

Such complex economic matters go frequently beyond the understanding—and largely beyond the control—of most of us, who simply want to live our individual lives, find meaningful work, support our families, and contribute to the common good the best that we can. Yet unless we happen to be entrepreneurs who launch out on our own to create new wealth (and jobs for others in the process), a great deal of our individual and family welfare—as well as our ability to contribute to society—comes down to our professional work.

For most of us, it's very basic: We need either a job or a better job.

Whether entry into the job market is voluntary or involuntary, making the effort to ensure the new job is the right fit is vital. Without it, we run the risk of being in another job search sooner than we need to be. The best solution is to take time to think about what you really want to do, developing a plan, then following through.

Transitions involve a thoughtful, methodical process, and this guide will help you step through it.

This book offers practical advice—along with job transition principles and skills—which will allow you to present yourself with as much human excellence as possible.

In terms assisting in the quest for a new or better job, this book has two overall purposes.

First, if you've lost your job, or looking for a change, this book will set you on the path to gaining an even better professional position. You want to work. You need to work. You value work. You enjoy work. At Hand & Associates, we've helped thousands before you, and this book will help you, too!

Second, whether you currently have a job or not, we'll show you the most effective method you can follow to provide the best long-term career insurance possible. Indeed, the process of career review, writing an achievement-style resume and well- focused cover letter, developing your success stories, enlisting the help of recruiters, preparing intensely for interviews, and understanding how to negotiate will all help you secure a new job at any time.

But above all, constant networking—in which you maintain a positive relationship with an ever-widening circle of contacts, colleagues, and friends for whom you prove sincere service whenever you can—will be your best long-term career "insurance."

This book is based on proven methods and resources for which topnotch clients have paid thousands of dollars to obtain. Now this knowledge is at your service—whether you're looking for a job, or have a job and are trying to find a better one. And as this book is based on timeless rather than faddish principles, it will be of value to you throughout your career.

Icons Used in This Book

Kevin's Handy Hints: In these sections, Kevin Hand offers us his personal advice on how to conduct the most effective, efficient, and impactful job search.

Attitude is Everything! None of us were born knowing about discipline, integrity, duty, persistence, and such. This symbol reminds us of qualities that contribute to our success.

CHAPTER 1: GETTING STARTED

"He has half the deed done who has made a beginning."— Horace

---

In This Chapter:
- ✓ *Realize that your new full time job (which you should start ASAP!) is finding a new job*
- ✓ *Take this time to prepare for a quality job search*
- ✓ *Envision your ideal job*

Searching for a job—regardless of circumstances leading up to the job hunt—can be stressful. With that said, knowing how challenging transitions may be, we recommend that you embrace it. Beginning your job search, much like beginning this book, can sometimes seem like a time-consuming and somewhat daunting task, however taking things one page at a time can lead you to an exciting new chapter.

We know how hard this time is for you. Yet we do not recommend that you waste a moment.

Our experience dictates that right now your time is best invested in a kind of personal retreat or self-conducted seminar. In these first days, you should take time to reflect deeply on who you are, what you can do and what you want. If you follow our counsel as taught in this and the next chapter, we guarantee that in just a few days you will emerge with a sense of your ideal job, a better appreciation of your transferable knowledge, and skills and the best resume you've ever written.

You'll be ready to launch your active job search.

How long should you wait to look for a job?

Sam, a 45-year-old man, was let go with a year's severance pay—a windfall that made his misfortune seem more bearable. Sam felt that in the past 20 years he had never taken any real time for himself and regretted it. He'd always wanted to travel, so he decided to take advantage of this opportunity and see a bit of the world.

At first, Sam intended to go away for a month. He had such a great time in France that he decided to stay away for just another month and see something of Italy. He felt a twinge of anxiety about putting off his job search back home, but heck, he thought, he still had his windfall income waiting for him.

As each month began to draw to a close, Sam decided to extend his trip a little longer. And each month he felt a nagging feeling about the future as his bank account shrank and his mental distance from the job market grew. After ten months, Sam had to return home nearly broke.

Now his anxiety—long suppressed—poured out. He both felt *and came across* as desperate to get a job. What was worse, when he had first left his previous position, he was on top of his game in terms of knowledge of his field and networking contacts. Now, after almost a year, both had cooled considerably.

It ended up taking Sam a full year to finally find another position. By then, he regretted what could have been. What if he'd started his job search right away and found a new position in three to four months, a realistic projection at that time? He could have landed the job, told his new boss up front that his start date would be one month later, then taken his vacation without a twinge of guilt—and began the new job with six months' wages in the bank!

When you're out of a job, how long should you wait to look for a new one?
You shouldn't wait a day, certainly not more than a week. There is no better time to start your new search than immediately.

Maintain a Routine

While employed, your company and job dictated how you spent a great deal of your time. Yet now you have a new full-time job: finding your next one.

We consider it imperative that you establish a workday routine. Just as when you were working for an employer, you need to get up at a set time, have a daily schedule, and go to bed at a reasonable hour so that you can continue your job search the following day. A routine which keeps you healthy, alert and productive is what you need right now to counter-balance the disorder that has been that has been thrown into your life.

Reflection: Taking a Fresh Look at Who You Are

As you begin this new phase in your professional life, you have two tasks:

The first is to reflect upon and record what you've accomplished in your career. Hopefully, you've been doing this all along and just need to update your records. If not, you now know that this is something which you could do from now on.

As with life itself, our careers go through various stages with growth, triumphs, setbacks and plateaus. At this moment, one could easily reflect with regret about this or that stage, moment, or decision. Our recommendation is for you to focus on the positive. To this end, it is essential that you capture and record your prior major job functions and your important accomplishments. It can be helpful to talk with family, friends and co-workers—and, yes, former bosses, too. Prepare a set of bullet points to record what job functions you have performed, along with brief qualitative descriptions, while not forgetting your achievements, with quantitative metrics wherever possible.

This kind of reflection and these types of recordings will not only make you feel good, but they will also give you the raw material necessary to write your achievement-style resume.

Your Ideal Job

Your second task in this new phase of your professional life is to dream about your ideal job. You do not want to just grab the first opportunity that presents itself or commit yourself to something that does not really appeal to you. Your ideal job is your goal, your touchstone. If you decide to accept anything less than your ideal, that is fine: you know what you are doing so you do not need to feel any regrets later.

The information you put together on your job functions and achievements list—along with your memories, impressions and lessons from the past—will help create a picture of the ideal job for you.

We suggest that you complete the Ideal Job exercise using the **Ideal Job** form reproduced at the end of this chapter. This exercise is designed to provide you with an image of what your ideal job might be, along with its environment, responsibilities and compensation.

In a sense, this ideal must take into account not only the best job for you but also the best you. That is to say, it simply cannot be a job wherein you do little work whilst reaping huge rewards; rather, it should be the job that most fully engages your own aspirations, talents, character strengths and skills.

The mental picture that this exercise can produce will be invaluable to you when you receive a job offer. The lure of a job offer often clouds our ability to see both the virtues and pitfalls of our impending new position. A few minutes of review at that moment can save you a whole lot of stress later. Thus, it is positively essential that you look back at what you envisioned as the ideal job at the beginning of your search.

Guideposts for your Journey

Over the years, through the extensive experience with our clients, Hand & Associates has identified certain steps you should take immediately. Analogously, we have learned that there are other things you should wait to do until you regain the clarity and equilibrium that the loss of a job may have temporarily taken away from you. Additionally, there are actions you should **never** perform because they would most assuredly hurt you **and** your search for a new position.

Unfortunately, what you might naturally *feel* like doing does not always correspond to what you *ought* to do. We, therefore, ask you to review the following Do's and Don'ts:

- **DO** talk with your loved ones; you need their support and it is important to keep them informed and discuss the short- and long-term implications of your career transition.

- **DO** reach out to trusted friends. Do this as a friend, not as someone expecting the friend to do something for you.

- **DO** take some time to process this experience. The loss of a job is rated by many as second to the loss of a spouse or child. A few days of rest can do wonders. However, while it is said that there are seven stages of grieving, you cannot wait for all the stages to be passed through. You have to get into the career transition process quickly so that you can maximize your recent experience and add the least disruption to your life.

- **DO** complete any work that you agreed to finish for your previous employer.

- **DO** review your telephone and cell phone messages to make sure they are thoroughly business-like. A phone message often serves as a potential employer's first impression of you. We suggest something straightforward such as:

   You've reached [Your FIRST and LAST NAME]. Please leave your name and number, and I will return your call as soon as possible. Thank you.

- **DO** take time to write down the key accomplishments, tasks and functions with which you were involved in your last position. It is amazing how quickly we minimize our accomplishments and how rapidly we even forget some of our most important work and contributions.

- **DO** only essential networking, contacting only those individuals and organizations that need to hear from you as to why you have left your position. For example, if you were working closely with a vendor or colleague at another company on a project, it is appropriate to let him or her know that you will no longer be involved. But remember: it is much wiser to develop a good resume and plan your networking and job-search strategy than to call everyone you know before you are prepared to present your best self to them.

And the DON'Ts, which may prove more important than the DOs:

- **DON'T** rush to talk to the companies in which you are most interested. We have the inclination to interview first with the companies that we view as high priority—often before we are really ready to interview effectively. Our first choice companies are the ones for which we have to be the most prepared. Take a lesson from entrepreneurs trying to raise venture capital: they might begin by making their pitches to investors they are pretty certain will not invest in their new company. Why? Simple: in order to polish their presentation and uncover the most common objections to it. Only then do they go to their most promising contacts.

- **DON'T** speak badly about your past employer, company, colleagues or products. Don't blame anyone or anything for your current situation. To do so makes you feel like a victim and makes you look sour to prospective employers.

- **DON'T** rush to talk to former competitors. Competitors may want to speak with you because they want to milk you for information or try to buy you "on the cheap." They understand that your stress and emotions may cloud your judgment. Remember, you want to speak as professionally about your former employers and colleagues as possible, since any prospective employer will assume that you might one day say about them what you are now saying about another company.

Moving Forward By Enlarging Your Potential Job Market

Now that we have helped you envision your ideal job, and given you some Do's and Don'ts in starting your journey, there's one more thing we suggest before beginning your resume: discover your transferable skills.

We are all endowed with abilities and skills. Once we articulate what these are—something which many people never do—we can use research, logic and imagination to envision where and how our skills and expertise can be employed in new ways.

Let's say that yesterday you worked in the communication, entertainment or financial sector, and today it seems there may be nowhere for you to go. But if you are good at analyzing numerical data, why couldn't you analyze data in an industry other than the one you are currently in? The same holds for a skill set like managing a project from start to finish. You know how to develop a budget, establish a timeline, put a roster of players in place, marshal resources, put the plan into effect, solve problems along the way, bring the project to completion, and analyze the results. That is a transferable skill.

We live in an age in which the development and diffusion of technology have created entirely new jobs, new companies, and even new industries. One example of diffusion of technology is home security systems. These have evolved from an alarm that simply bleats inside your house to a comprehensive system that allows you to watch what's going on at home in real-time video which is captured by cameras, sent to microwave towers and received on your cell phone.

Chapter 1: Getting Started

With the transferability of your skills, you could be a player in new arenas.

Use the **Transferable Skills** form at the end of this chapter to identify and begin to evaluate how each element of your skill and expertise set could be expanded into other areas.

Once you've recorded your past job functions and achievements, envisioned your ideal job and isolated your transferable skills, it's time to write your achievement-style resume. Chapter Two will teach you everything you need in order to write the best resume of your career.

Personal responsibility. Honesty. Respect for others. Courage in undertaking initiatives and in enduring difficulties. Self-control. Sound decision-making. Order and good use of time. Generosity and self-sacrifice. Gratitude for blessings. Loyalty to one's family, friends, employee, and country. Industriousness.

These and other human virtues are absolutely necessary for us to live fulfilling lives.

What are virtues? Virtues are stable habits which define our character. A respectful person, for example, is one who treats each person he encounters with dignity. A courageous person is one who does the right thing even when experiencing fear. A generous person is able to give of himself when called upon or whenever he sees a real need.

To do our professional work well, we have to develop a whole series of human virtues such as the ones enumerated above. Mature adults can acquire natural virtues by understanding what they are and practicing them over and over.

There are dozens of human virtues. In subsequent chapters, we will touch on a few of the key virtues as they relate to your job search.

The IDEAL JOB

ORGANIZATION
In what business or industry would you prefer to work?

_____

_____

_____

RESPONSIBILITIES
Describe your ideal scope of responsibility:

_____

_____

_____

COMPANY CULTURE
Describe the values and ethics of an organization you'd enjoy:

_____

_____

_____

MANAGEMENT STYLE
List daily business approaches you'd like a new employer to possess:

_____

_____

_____

COMPENSATION
What would be your preferred job package and salary?

_____

_____

DAY-TO-DAY
Describe a typical day at your ideal job:

_____

_____

_____

The **TRANSFERRABLE SKILLS** Form

When you have completed this form, review your skills and consider how they may be used in other fields, careers, or industries that interest you.

ANALYTICAL SKILLS: Working with DATA & INFORMATION
Includes evaluation and manipulation of data and information such as budgets, planning, organization, solutions, and providing interpretations.

_____

_____

_____

_____

CONCEPTUAL SKILLS: Working with IDEA
Includes researching, creating, describing, developing, and implementing projects, systems, and procedures.

_____

_____

_____

_____

PEOPLE SKILLS: Working with PEOPLE
Includes management, training, mentoring, coaching, and team-related activities.

_____

_____

_____

_____

SPECIAL SKILLS
Includes unique and specialized abilities (i.e., artistic or financial skills), political acumen within organizations, PR skills, etc.

_____

_____

_____

_____

CHAPTER 2: YOUR RESUME

"If you have done it, it ain't bragging."— Walt Whitman

In This Chapter:
- ✓ *Take control of your Internet presence*
- ✓ *Organize and record past major job functions and achievements*
- ✓ *Expand your horizons to imagine the different types of work you could be doing in the future*
- ✓ *Brainstorm and list other achievements that may be pertinent to your desired position*

Your Unofficial Resume

Before the Internet became a popular tool for hiring managers, first impressions were obtained from a piece paper over which you had complete control. However, with a world of information available through the Internet, decision makers today can simply type in your name to learn more about you.

It is important that you know what is showing up in online searches about you, so you need to do a search on your own name. What comes up? Think about what you would want a prospective employer to see and compare it to everything the search has pulled up about you. Be sure to review any social pages you have on sites such as LinkedIn, Facebook, Pinterest, and YouTube.

Now, take control! First, on sites where you can post a profile (having a LinkedIn account is highly recommended), make sure it is complete and up-to-date. Next, try to edit or delete any uncomplimentary posts (you may have to do an Internet search for instructions on how to do so). Then start adding digital information to create the best possible picture for others to see. Start a blog and add to it regularly. Post articles about your field or specialty. Participate in a forum related to your industry or interests. **Build a positive online presence.**

That being said, it is still necessary to create a traditional resume.

Job Finding Logic:
1. Resumes get you interviews, not jobs.
2. Interviews get jobs.
    People get jobs by how well they can sell themselves utilizing their success stories.

Writing Your Resume

Writing a resume is a recursive process. This means that it requires brainstorming, drafting, reflecting, rewriting, and revising.

In writing your resume you are learning to tell your own story. While the resume does not consist of your "success stories"—which you will work on in Chapter Four—it does represent the broad sweep of your career thus far. You need to understand this big picture yourself, which is why you should write your own resume, even if you were to have an employment counselor assist you. For example, one educational administrator did not realize that the pattern of her career consisted of moving from smaller to larger schools and, consequently, from lesser to greater responsibilities. The big picture did not click into place for her until she worked on her resume. When she saw the pattern, it became easy for her to explain why she moved from one job to another, and this career progression became a powerful positive factor in her job search.

A hiring manager (i.e., the person who interviews you and has the power to offer you a job) may receive tens, hundreds, even thousands of resumes. Remember, a resume can make you stand out in the crowd, capturing the reader's attention and leading to an initial interview. But how can your resume motivate this hiring manager to contact you?

In this chapter, we'll teach you how to write a specific kind of resume: the achievement-style resume. It is a continuing consensus that the achievement-style resume gets interviews more often than any other resume. In fact, the ratio is 20 to 1 over the traditional pure job-description resume.

6 Seconds to Make an Impression

According to a number of recent studies, recruiters spend about 6 seconds to review a resume. **Six seconds**! Therefore, you must portray yourself as clearly and attractively as possible to get as much as you can out of the little time you have:

- Use bullets of information that are concise and powerful
- Bold headers to divide your resume into clear sections for easier navigation through the information

The Achievement-Style Resume

An achievement-style resume is a chronological summary of your experience. Like many authorities on resume-writing, we believe that presenting the last 10 to 15 years of your accomplishments and experience is the best way to showcase yourself. Once you start the interview process, you can discuss earlier work experience if you think such will help.

The achievement-style resume is a form of persuasive writing. It makes a claim and then supports this claim. On your resume, you are focusing on your positive achievements and presenting yourself as a high-achiever who can help your potential employer.

Structuring Your Resume

The achievement-style resume has four parts:

1. Contact information
2. Your "Who I Am" statement
3. A list of positions held over the past 10 to 15 years with achievement bullet-points supporting your "Who I Am" statement
4. Other significant achievements such as education, training, and awards

Below we explain each of the four parts in detail to assist as you develop, revise and refine your own achievement- style resume.

1. **Contact Information**

   Provide this information at the top of the first page, including your name, city, state, and email address. Include a phone number if you are comfortable doing so. We also recommend adding your LinkedIn profile URL where the hiring manager can go to get a more in-depth picture of you.

2. **The "Who I Am" Statement**

   This is the most important statement of your entire resume. The "Who I Am" is a stand-alone snapshot of you in two or three concise, high-impact sentences. It is a 1 such, it sets a limit or parameter to your search. Rather than focusing on what you want, the "Who I Am" statement discusses the skills you bring to the table, revealing who you are and what you can offer your potential employer.

   <u>Mastering the "Who I Am" Statement</u>

   The "Who I Am" statement is structured to deliver a high-impact, concise vision of your expertise, your occupational breadth and your major strengths. The ideal statement consists of two or three sentences: first a sentence of what you do and then one or two sentences of your strengths.

   Note that you should use a third sentence only if your strengths and skills extend that far. Also, technically, these are sentence fragments—you are leaving out the "I am" or the "I have" because they are understood.

   First Sentence: A one-sentence description of you containing a descriptive title or phrase, years of experience, and type of company and industry or industry-sector.

   > Example: A Vice-President of Marketing with 15 years' experience in both small and large food processing companies.

   > *Effect:* This statement claims you can do anything a highly experienced marketing executive in the food processing business can do.

   Second Sentence: A statement of your major strengths and expertise.

   > Example: Proven ability to penetrate new markets and expand existing business opportunities using state-of-the-art strategic planning and research methods.

   > *Effect:* This statement claims that you can help grow a company by planning and research.

Third Sentence (optional): If appropriate, a second statement of strengths or skills.

Example: Skilled in developing, directing and coordinating a strong national marketing team and a fast-moving sales force.

Effect: This statement claims that you can lead a team which will market and sell on a national basis.

Put these three together, and they look like this:

A Vice-President of Marketing with 15 years of experience in both small and large food processing companies. Proven ability to penetrate new markets and expand existing business opportunities using state-of-the-art strategic planning and research methods. Skilled in developing, directing and coordinating a strong national marketing team and a fast-moving sales force.

We recommend that you avoid the use of weak sweeping terms such as:

Aggressive	Energetic	Self-Starter
Challenging	Go-Getter	Strong Communicator
Creative	Hard Worker	Team Player
Detail-Oriented	High-Energy	Workaholic
Dynamic	On-Time	

Additional Examples of "Who I Am" Statements

- A film editor with over 10 years' experience on two dozen major Hollywood features and low-budget independent films. A pioneer in using and teaching non-linear editing systems. Extensive experience in cutting-edge pre-visual and post-production digital editing.

- A degree-certified primary-level teacher with 10 years' experience in multi-cultural classrooms. Leadership in implementing a standards-based curriculum. Proven ability to meet the needs of diverse learners.

- A Vice President of Human Resources with 16 years of experience in a large company in the publishing industry. Major strengths include the ability to avoid union presence in large organizations through creative benefits program. Highly skilled in negotiating and managing contracts and plans across diverse groups of employers.

- A logistics, material management and strategic planning professional with a demonstrated track record of reducing expenses while significantly improving service standards. Strong technical skills and extensive experience enhanced by advanced education in logistics and management.

3. Career Achievements

Your career achievements support your "Who I Am" statements. Each of your "career achievements" has a two-part structure. The first part is a particular career experience—a job—and the second consists of career achievements bullet points.

Beginning with the most recent job, list each employer by company name and location, your last position held, and years of service. As stated earlier, limit this section of your resume to your last 10 to 15 years of work.

Note: Always show the beginning year to "Present" for the most **recent** job. This indicates there is no gap in your employment record.

Next, list your achievements with this company in bullet points. You started this task in the last chapter. Construct your bullets with an eye to maximizing your value to other employers and to other types of businesses. Present your skills in a manner that demonstrates your versatility and ability to have a value outside your current position and industry.

Whenever possible, always quantify your achievements. Use dollar values, percentage increases, savings in productivity, sales or other volume measurement. The reason is that numbers are usually accepted as objective facts, not overblown subjective assertions.

For example, "Trained west coast sales force" is a lower-impact, purely qualitative achievement. "Trained west coast sales force which achieved 50% higher sales than all other regional sales forces," however, is a high-impact quantitative achievement. Great to use if you can claim it!

The number of bullets per job partly depends on the number of years in that position and to some extent on your prior positions, and then on the number and value of prior accomplishments. Generally, three bullets per position is a good number.

Note: Keep in mind that how you accomplished the achievement should be left for success stories which you use in your networking and interviewing. This will be taught in Chapter Four.

When constructing your achievement bullet points, **use** specific, active terms including (more terms are listed in Appendix A):

Directed	Lowered	Reduced
Implemented	Organized	Renewed
Improved	Prepared	Saved
Increased	Recovered	Trained

Full Example

ABC TRANSIT– Los Angeles, CA   **2003–Present**
Regional Manager
- Increased division sales by 30% during the first year of service followed by a steady increase of 10% annually in subsequent years.
- Saved $2MM over two years by developing a new computerized distribution system.
- Reduced staff from 45 to 26 by introducing a new PC-based tracking system.

More About Achievement Bullet-Points

When quantifying achievements, use the measure that gives the greatest impact.

- If the absolute numbers are small, try another indicator, such as a percentage, which may be more impressive. For example, increasing output of something by 50% may sound better than from five to ten.
- A statement of achievement in the past is usually higher impact than one which is still on-going, because it appears to be proven. A statement in the present and continuing into the future can appear to be incomplete and theoretically unproven.
- As a general rule, placement of achievements goes from the most powerful first to the least powerful last. You want to front-load achievements because the reader may only be scanning your resume.
- List one achievement per bullet. Do not combine them.
- If you do not have measurable accomplishments, then highlight qualitative experience and functional skills which establish leadership, competence and innovation. Examples include:
  - Administered a 400-bed hospital
  - Managed 37 people

- Led four teams
- Created a new wellness program to enhance employee satisfaction and improve attendance
- Wrote Q & A protocol for customer service representatives

Where to look for quantifiable results:

Accounting: Improvements that shortened time lags in billing, reporting and providing financial data

Marketing: Increased sales volume and/or market share
New market penetrations
New product introductions

Sales: Increased sales volume in existing markets
Increased market share

Production: Increased unit production
Reduction in operating expenses
Reduction in scrap and rework
Reduction in overtime

Purchasing: Decrease in out-of-stock items
Lower inventory losses
Lower cost of materials and services

Info Systems: Reduction in "Out-of-Stock" times for production or sales
Improved cost control

4. Other Achievements: Education & Training or Seminars

This final section of your achievement-style resume is optional, depending on what you have or do not have to include. Here you note impressive educational degrees, special training, awards, honors, and notable achievements.

In most professional careers, a college degree and even an advanced degree is expected or essential. We suggest leaving off the year of graduation unless you have worked less than five years.

Achievements that you might consider to include are college or career honors, grants or fellowships, recognition or awards, appointments or volunteer service, and military service. The key is that you consider what value the award or activity will have in the professional world. For example, if you graduated first in your class with a MA in Classics, that is certainly appropriate if you are pursuing a teaching position, but it may have no relevance if you want to lead a sales force.

A helpful exercise is to begin by chronicling lifetime achievements to determine those which are appropriate to catalogue in a resume, those which can be talked about in an interview, and those which are irrelevant for particular jobs. The **Lifetime Achievements–Memory Jogger** form at the end of this chapter should be helpful in this regard.

The ideal length of a resume is one or two pages. An executive with unique or complex career accomplishments may merit a third page, but this should be done only when the content of the bullets merit that much space. Remember the purpose of your resume: to get an interview, not a job. Therefore, you only want to put enough information into the resume to prompt the reader to contact you.

Delivering Your Resume

When you finish the first draft of your resume, you are not yet ready to send it out. You are not even ready to send it out even when you have polished it to perfection. Why? Because you still need to write cover letters, develop and master your success stories, research companies which you will be contacting, study interviewing techniques, and begin networking.

The growth of email has definitely triggered a movement towards accepting resumes by electronic means only. Normally, you should embed your cover letter in the text of the email and attach your resume. (Cover letter writing is taken up in the next chapter.) Furthermore, we suggest that you save your resume as a PDF so that all formatting is maintained.

Standing Out From The Crowd

While email is by far the prevailing method of communication in most companies, many executives have told us that they mail their resumes or provide a copy in person whenever it is permissible. These professionals understand that emailed resumes are easier to dispose of with less reading or reviewed by staff, and they often get less exposure to the hiring authority. We recommend, in order to stand out in this digital age, to submit the resume electronically and follow up by mailing a hard copy of the cover letter and resume later on.

Responsibility is the stable disposition of giving others what you owe them. A responsible person carries out his or her duties and obligations fully. Further, responsibility includes accepting the consequences of one's own actions.

There are responsibilities associated with your job, as well as other roles you may have such as family member and volunteer. A responsible person looks at every situation and asks, "What is my duty?" and then does it.

Responsible isn't a very 'sexy' quality, but it is the first virtue you have to develop if you want to be a competent, valuable employee.

Two important questions to consider are: "What is my responsibility right now?" and "Am I fulfilling it?" Are you giving your employer his due, or do you need to reevaluate your intentions? If you don't have a job, are you using your time well knowing that your current job is finding a job?

Sample Resume

BOB SMITH, CIA

Chicago, IL ● (123) 456-7890 ● YourName@gmail.com ● www.linkedin.com/in/sample123

Certified Internal Auditor with over 15 years of experience in financial, operational and compliance auditing in the healthcare industry. Excellent oral and written communication skills resulting in obtaining financial recoveries and implementing procedural changes. Interfaces effectively with all levels of management.

Career Achievements

123 HEALTH Co. — Los Angeles, CA   2004 – Present
Disbursement Auditor (2011 - Present)
Performed financial and compliance audits of disbursement systems. Reviewed regional procurement and travel cards to ensure compliance with policies and procedures. Performed contract reviews of material and supply vendors, resulting in reimbursement for pricing discrepancies.

- Discovered $370K in overpayments through the review of cost plus contracts.
- Recovered $30K in overcharges due to external vendors not passing along cost savings. Contract terminology was added to all purchasing contracts to ensure the ability to perform audits and recover possible overcharges.

Internal Auditor (2004 - 2011)
Responsible for planning and performing financial, compliance and operational audits. Performed all phases of audit process from the preliminary review through the final report.

- Responsibilities also included the supervision of other auditors and the coordination of findings to all levels of management.
- Performed a review of the regional dues revenue system. Identified $364K in delinquent dues, which were subsequently recovered. Recommended procedures to verify correctness of dues payments.

LA COUNTY CONTROLLER'S OFFICE — Los Angeles, CA   2001 – 2004
Staff Internal Auditor
Supervised and performed operational and financial audits at four different Los Angeles County hospitals. Identified and developed audit areas, developed and wrote audit programs, trained new audit staff and drafted reports to hospital management.

- Assisted in the development of a new billing system for Rancho Vallarta Hospital. Reduced the number of days outstanding in accounts receivable.
- Conducted a contract review of a private hospital, which provides care for Los Angeles County patients. Audit findings disclosed overpayments of $20K.

Education & Training

Bachelor of Science – Business Administration
Pepperdine University, Malibu, CA
Rich Edmund Course Graduate

Affiliations

Member, Institute of Internal Audits
Member, Association of Healthcare Internal Auditors

The RESUME DEVELOPMENT Form

THE "WHO I AM" STATEMENT

The "Who I Am" statement consists of two or three sentences:
(1) A description of yourself which contains—a descriptive title or phrase; years of experience; and type of company and industry or industry-sector.
(2) A statement of your major strengths and expertise. And, if warranted,
(3) a second statement of exceptional skills or major strengths.

_____

_____

_____

_____

CAREER ACCOMPLISHMENTS

Starting with the most recent job, complete the following section for each position held in the past 10 to 15 years.

Employer: _____

City, State: _____ From/To: _____

Title: _____

Brief description of responsibilities:

_____

_____

_____

List 3 to 4 achievements (quantifiable, if possible):

- _____

  _____

- _____

  _____

- _____

  _____

- _____

  _____

EDUCATION (Complete for each degree held)

Degree: _____

College/University: _____

City, State: _____

PROFESSIONAL LICENSURE & CERTIFICATIONS

Professional License: _____

License or Certification: _____

TRAINING/SEMINARS

_____

_____

_____

PROFESSIONAL ASSOCIATIONS

_____

_____

_____

The LIFETIME ACHIEVEMENTS-MEMORY JOGGER Form

Examples of achievements are listed below. Work through the following categories and circle any item that applies to you. adding any experience you may have had that is not on the list. Do not include personal interests, salary history, religion, or comments about health or references.

ACADEMIC RECOGNITION

- Dean's List
- Graduation Recognition (i.e., Cum Laude)
- Unique Scholarships/Grants
- Fellowships (i.e., Rhodes, Scholar)
- Other: _____

WORK-RELATED ACCOMPLISHMENTS

- Customer Service Excellence Award
- Awards for making Significant Suggestions
- Appointments to Special or Select Committees or Teams
- Awards for System Creation/Development and Implementation
- Awards for Creating and/or Developing Procedures
- Awards for Cost Savings
- Other: _____

PUBLIC SERVICE AWARDS/NATIONAL RECOGNITION

- Service or Award for National/State/Major City Commission
- Participation/Winner/Nominee in a major award program such as industry awards, arts and performance awards
- Appointment or winning placement on National Team
- Founded non-profit/association/club
- Other: _____

MISCELLANEOUS

- _____
- _____
- _____

CHAPTER 3: COVER LETTERS

"This letter is longer than usual because I lacked the time to write a shorter one."— Blaise Pascal

In This Chapter:
- ✓ *A good cover letter motivates the reader to move on to your resume.*
- ✓ *The best kind of cover letter is tailored for a specific position using the "Mirror" technique.*
- ✓ *A generic cover letter is appropriate when you cannot get details about the position, or are not targeting a specific job.*
- ✓ *If you have one major strength or accomplishment, write a cover letter using the "Big Gun" approach.*

It is estimated that less than 50% of cover letters are ever read. At the same time, according to a recent survey by CareerBuilder.com, 66% of hiring managers prefer an appropriate cover letter with a resume. And there are some employers who prefer a cover letter in lieu of a resume!

It is, therefore, necessary to write the most effective cover letter possible. The benefit to you—the job hunter—is that you get to practice stating your case one more time, regardless of what happens to the letter.

The cover letter is meant to draw the reader's attention like the headline of a newspaper story. With this in mind, we amend the "job-finding logic" from the previous chapter as follows:

The design of your cover letter affects both whether someone will read the resume and what he or she will get from it. In other words, it is not simply the content of your cover letter but how that content is presented. We recommend using short, bullet points to highlight your job functions and successes so the reader is more likely to see what you most wanted to impart.

Job Finding Logic:
1. The cover letter gets someone to read your resume.
2. Your resume leads to an interview.
3. The interview gets someone to hire you.

Types of Cover Letters

Hand & Associates advocates the use of two types of bullet-based cover letters: the generic and the "mirror" cover letters. (Samples of each can be found at the end of this chapter.)

"Mirror" Cover Letters

The "mirror" technique provides a great way to respond to an ad for any position. This letter is custom written for a specific company and position, and responds to what you have learned about the job. It informs the reader that you "mirror" the requirements and experience sought for the job being offered. The mirror letter is preferred whenever you can write one.

If you possess the qualifications as outlined in the advertisement or from information you gathered through research, there is no more effective way to demonstrate this than by using the "mirror" technique. This method virtually assures that your resume will be read, because the reviewer will see the match between you and the job.

The mirror cover letter demonstrates to a potential employer that you care enough about this opportunity to personally tailor your letter to respond to the ad or information provided.

Further, it is the perfect vehicle for highlighting the parts of your resume that would be of greatest interest to this employer. By drawing attention to a different combination of qualifications in each cover letter, you can appear to be an ideal candidate to a wide variety of employers without having to reinvent your resume for each opportunity.

Chapter 3: Cover Letters

<u>Generic Cover Letters</u>

The generic cover letter provides a general summary of your career, as well as your major strengths and accomplishments. This letter can be used as an inquiry to a company you are interested in but don't know enough about the position to write a mirror or response letter.

A majority of the time, resumes are sent via email, and as mentioned earlier, the cover letter should be incorporated into the body of the email with the resume attached. As such, the cover letter consists of (1) a salutation; (2) an opening statement; (3) achievement/functional bullet points; (4) a closing. We also recommend that the subject of the email includes the name of the job for which you are applying.

1. **Salutation**

   Ideally, the letter should be addressed to the hiring manager. If you are sending the letter to someone unknown, the proper way to address the salutation is "Dear Sir or Madam:".

2. **Opening Statement**

   The opening sentence of most cover letters should quickly address who you are. For example, "I am a consumer products Marketing Director with over 10 years' experience in the entertainment industry."

3. **Achievement/Functional Bullets:**

   The advantage of a one-sentence opening is that it allows the reader to immediately jump to your bullet points. These key points are based on your experience (which can be work and volunteer related) and showcase your skills, without simply repeating what is in your resume.

   Examples:

   - Developed the marketing strategy which increased product impressions by 175%.
   - Identified, negotiated and implemented cooperative cross-marketing agreements which resulted in a 100% increase in cooperative advertising, worth over $2MM in advertising exposure.

   Notice how each of the above bullet points identifies a function and specific achievement using statistics to show concrete results.

   Don't panic if your occupation or industry does not lend itself to quantifiable achievements. Purely function-based bullets can be effective for cover letters, so create bullets that are the most relevant to the potential employer. For example, "Administered 120 bed, 30-staff psychiatric residential facility." Likewise, if you don't have impressive achievements, focus on your functions and your skills in carrying them out.

4. Closing

The closing of your cover letter should be short and specific, thanking them for their consideration and stating your desire to have the reader contact you for an interview.

Resume Request Cover Letter

If you are fortunate enough to have someone contact you asking for your resume, you should send it with a cover letter.

If the request is from someone you know, your cover letter should be short and to the point. The letter should include a thank you for the resume request and, where appropriate, a statement sending your good wishes to the individual and his or her family if you know them.

If the request is from a recruiter or potential employer, you should treat this as a formal request. The body of the letter should be no more than a paragraph or two, the first being the thank you portion and the second being a brief statement of your interest in the position and that you are available for an interview.

Example:

I would like to thank you for requesting that I send you my resume.

Your company is of great interest to me, and I am looking forward to the chance to meet with you soon to explore how my experience can be put to profitable use by your Internet start-up venture.

The "Big Gun" Cover Letter

If you have one dominant achievement that's so impressive that you want to get to it immediately, fire your biggest gun—your most impressive achievement—right in the first sentence of your letter.

When using this technique, hiring managers might call just to hear your secret to success. While it may seem that the big gun approach to the cover letter is of use only to someone who has an exceptional achievement to hang his or her hat on, the truth is that anyone can use the big gun strategy.

If you cannot think of a specific and measurable accomplishment that seems to qualify as your "big achievement," you are probably not thinking hard enough. Any work experience that can be quantified and expressed with specific, measurable results will do.

- As sales manager of Tarrytown Motors, I led our small team to increase our fleet sales 30% per year for three years in a row.
- I raised $750,000 for Willow Grove Country Day School last year.

If you have trouble thinking of a predominant achievement, then substitute that with the predominant "theme" of your career. This could be your most outstanding quality, such as creativity or dependability, illustrated by specific achievements based on this quality:

- As an intensive care nurse at Meadview Community Hospital, I was awarded the "Most Compassionate Caregiver."
- During my two years playing minor league ball for the Yorkshire Big Apples before my knee injury, I had the reputation of being the smartest player in the franchise, something I can bring to Alabama U's baseball program as head coach.

Your predominant achievement could also be your main area of specialization or expertise.

- In the maintenance department, I proved myself to be "the" go-to guy in terms of engine troubleshooting.

Or your predominant achievement could simply be a major problem you helped solve for your previous employer, along with the specific results your solution helped to achieve.

- After studying the issue, I designed and operated a system which managed our customer orders, vendors, inventory, and shipping and billing, saving the company $20,000 per year.

If you can determine the biggest need, want, problem or goal of the potential employer, and you have a major achievement or specialized skill in that area, give the precise details in your cover letter.

Cover Letter Content – General Guidelines

In writing your cover letter, you need to stay focused on what you want the cover letter to accomplish. More specifically:

- **Remember your strategy.** You want a short letter designed to focus on your strengths, allowing for a rapid evaluation of your merits.

- **Mirror the reader's needs.** Whenever possible, design your letter and, in particular, your bullets to match the potential employer's needs. The letter should seek to answer in the briefest form for the employer, "What's in it for me?"

- **Match the reader's wavelength whenever possible.** If possible, try to ascertain the reader's temperament, as well as the character and culture of the potential employer. In essence, the letter seeks to tune into the company's mindset.

- **Use good judgment in analyzing the employer's needs.** Look at how the ad information is listed or how it is orally presented to you. Often, the sequence is based on the employer's judgment of the needs or priorities for the position. These may be listed in descending order of importance or some kind of logical sequence. When you match these needs, follow their presented sequence. When you do not have an exact match, place the most powerful matching skills first.

- **Keep it consistent.** Match the heading of your cover letter to the one of your resume. On the off chance the two get separated, using the same format to provide your name and contact information at the top of the page makes the documents recognizable as a set.

- **Be interesting.** By being interesting, we're not implying that you write in a jazzy style or that you present what you consider to be your greatest attributes. We mean that you should be interesting to the reader. How so? The reader is interested in you as someone who can meet his or her needs. Claim you can meet those needs and you will be interesting.

- **Specifics are much more effective than generalities.** Specific percentages, numbers and other numerical values and quantitative phrases should be utilized wherever possible. See Appendix A: Resume Action Words for terms which will help generate effective phrases.

- **Cover letters should allude to your knowledge and expertise.** A reader of your letter may want to meet you if he or she believes you can offer information either about the industry or aspects of your craft because of how you presented your accomplishments and experience.

- **Keep it simple.** Avoid stilted language, long sentences and the passive voice.

> Passive voice: "Sales were increased by 27%."
> Active Voice: "Increased sales by 27%."

Taboos of Cover-Letter Writing

It is important that you do not surrender any information that might be used either to eliminate you from consideration or compromise your ability to negotiate later.

- **Don't provide salary information.** As a general rule, it is not wise to include salary information—either salary history or your expected salary for this position—even when it is requested or 'required.' It is better to deal with salary information during the interview to retain the opportunity for negotiation.

- **Don't reveal why you are looking for a new position.** The cover letter is not the place to discuss this subject.

- **Don't overstate your achievements and experience.** Since eventually the truth will reveal itself, a cover letter based on exaggeration—or even lies—will only waste everyone's time and destroy your reputation.

- **When presenting a hardcopy, never use corporate stationary, colored stationary or paper with designs.** Letters typewritten on quality white paper are universally recognized as professional and business-like.

- **Never address someone you do not know by his or her first name.** The reader may be appreciate your informality.

Final Tips on Cover Letters:

Before typing the cover letter directly into your email, type it out in a Word document and save it to your hard drive. Doing this will ensure you do not send an incomplete cover letter by mistake and will give you plenty of time to write a letter-perfect cover. In addition, sometimes computer glitches cause you to lose part, or all, of you work. Instead, when your letter is ready, copy it from the original and paste it in the email message window. Even though Microsoft Word's SpellCheck can be incredibly helpful, you will still need to proofread this new version and correct any unwanted formatting changes or losses which occurred by pasting it onto the email. Don't forget to attach your resume.

Before sending off the material to your potential employer, we suggest that you also email this package to yourself to test how it looks and whether everything opens properly.

Loyalty is an essential trait in every relationship of importance—spouses to one another, parents to children and children to parents, friends to friends, employers to employees, employees to employers, citizens to their country, and so on.

We have said that a job seeker should never bad-mouth anyone they have encountered in their career. Neither should confidential information be revealed. When we follow these simple guidelines, we are being loyal. As a loyal employee, you earn respect—from your employer and co-workers—which will follow you wherever you go.

A loyal person remains committed despite any discomfort he may encounter. He is also faithful to his commitments and obligations.

It is good to ask yourself if you are loyal to your family, employer, and friends. Are you willing to put their needs ahead of your own? While it is fair to assume you will gain their loyalty in return, it is not something you do with the expectation of getting something in return.

Sample "Mirror" Cover Letters

Growing Los Angeles Software company seeks CFO with 10-15 years of experience. Experience with middle market a must. Corporate management background essential. CPA required. Software company experience a big plus. Salary 100K plus bonus and stock options.

The following is a cover letter sent in response to the advertisement above. Here, John Citizen can address his email to a specific person since it was listed in the job posting.

Re: **Chief Financial Officer—Wall Street Journal Posting**

Dear Mr. Smith,

I have been a financial executive for the past 16 years, the last eight with a $90MM maker of computer hard drives. My strengths include developing innovative ways to make financial data accessible to front-line managers for use in daily decisions.

Further qualifications which provide a good match for your advertised position include:

- Extensive middle market company experience.
- Experience as a Controller for a Silicon Valley software developer serving the engineering marketplace.
- CPA from New York University, graduating cum laude.

I appreciate the opportunity to speak with you about the position and I look forward to hearing from you soon.

Sincerely,

John Citizen

Five years proven experience in store management with the ability to train people and to provide leadership in expanding the organization.

Re: **Pet Store Manager—Indeed**

Dear Sir or Madam:

I have been a pet store manager for over 10 years with a track record of increasing sales in excess of inflation for every year since my arrival.

My experience includes:

- Hiring, training and supervising a staff of up to 10 individuals, with a retention rate that averages over three years per employee.
- Increasing profitability of the operation for the last six years.

- Leading opening team for four of the chain's 10 retail stores, providing manager training, hiring assistance, training in marketing and grand-opening advertising campaigns.

Attached is my resume, which highlights my employment history and achievements. I look forward to hearing from you and appreciate your consideration.

Sincerely,

A leader with a proven track record and the ability to train and to provide input and leadership in developing new products to meet market needs.

Re: **Regional Sales Manager—LinkedIn Jobs**

Dear Sir or Madam:

I am a Regional Sales Manager for a major consumer productions manufacturer with over eight years' experience, increasing sales from $2.5MM to $35MM during that time.

My successes include:

- Conceived, developed and implemented a regional sales and expense containment plan that resulted in the highest ROI and profitability for any region. The entire corporation has adopted this plan.
- Managed and directed the efforts of a 12-member sales force with an average sales increase of over 10% per salesperson over the last three years.
- Provided the initial input and led efforts to develop a unique new PDA system that returned the largest first-year ROI of any new product in the company's history.

I appreciate your consideration and look forward to hearing from you soon.

Sincerely,

Sample Generic Cover Letters

Re: **Marketing Director position**

Dear Mr. Jones,

I am a consumer products Marketing Director with over 10 years' experience in the entertainment industry. Expertise and accomplishments include:

- Developing the marketing strategy which increased product impressions by 175%.
- Identifying, negotiating and implementing cooperative cross-marketing agreements which resulted in a 100% increase in cooperative advertising, worth over $2MM in advertising exposure.
- Creating marketing teams which learned from the sales force and clients, resulting in a new product yielding over $1MM in sales in its first year of production.

Enclosed is my resume. I would appreciate an opportunity to discuss my qualifications with you regarding this position. Thank you for your consideration.

Cordially,

The following example highlights job functions in lieu of achievements:

Re: **VP for Information Technology position**

Dear Sir or Madam:

I am a decisive and results-oriented Information Technology Executive. I have over 15 years of experience optimizing an organization's information technology environment through cogent analysis and efficient deployment of cost-effective, reliable and secure architecture, business processes and training.

Expertise includes:

- Input in developing strategic business plans and directing the alignment of the IT strategy's architecture and organization to meet immediate and long-term plan goals.
- Optimization of current hardware and software asset utilization through business process modification and/or prudent capital investment.
- Leadership in a difficult business environment, such as in pre/post-acquisition, corporate leadership change, adverse market conditions or new financial constraints.

Enclosed is my resume for your review. I would appreciate an opportunity to discuss my qualifications with you. Thank you for your consideration.

Sincerely,

Sample "Big Gun" Cover Letter

Notice how much more powerful John Citizen's "big gun" cover letter compares to the "mirror" cover letter he wrote for the same position:

Re: Chief Financial Officer—Wall Street Journal Posting

Dear Mr. Smith,

In my last eight years as a stock broker, my annual gross production has never been less than $800K and is usually closer to my high of $1.25MM, reached in the banner year of 2005.

But even in this "leaner and meaner" era on Wall Street, I have turned in a superb performance, averaging about $1MM in gross commission production.

Part of the reason I have been a top producer for the firm is that I have given my clients a highly personal and caring level of service that has kept them fiercely loyal to me.

I would welcome the opportunity to share with you the strategies I have found so successful in this investment marketplace, strategies which have been directly responsible for my being the number one producer in my office for the last four years running.

I will call on Thursday morning to see if you have an interest in setting up an interview. In the meantime, if you have any questions, I may be reached at (444) 555-6666.

Sincerely,

John Citizen

CHAPTER 4: YOUR SUCCESS STORIES

"The only source of knowledge is experience."— Albert Einstein

In This Chapter:
- ✓ *Success stories are what you sue to describe your accomplishments orally*
- ✓ *Each success story illustrates one of your achievement bullet-points from your resume*
- ✓ *Each story should take about a minute to relate, but not more than two*
- ✓ *Program your success stories into your memory so that you can instantly and spontaneously recall them*

The purpose of a resume is to get you an interview, a subject which will be discussed in great depth in Chapters Seven and Eight.

In order to prepare for discussions about points listed in your resume, you need to develop your success stories. It is vital that you have a clear picture of how you will respond upon and expand the claims you have put forth.

Depending on the depth of your experience, you may have one or several success stories. A success story is a description of how you achieved one of the successes you cited in your resume.

Job Search Logic:

- Your "Who I Am" statement in your resume is a series of claims about you.
- Your achievement-style bullet points in your resume support those claims.
- Your success stories expand upon those bullet points.

Developing Your Success Stories

You develop your success story by first writing it out and then practicing it verbally until you can flawlessly relate it. While it may not be necessary for you to have a success story for each achievement, it is essential that the most complex and interesting achievements have success stories to support them.

A success story should consist of no more than two minutes of spoken comment. This means approximately 100-180 words. Write your success story in an oral—not formal written—style because you will eventually be speaking it.

Achievement-Style Bullet Points and Corresponding Success Stories

Example #1—Your resume's bullet point reads what you did:

- Grew the enrollment of the summer program by 50% and increased net profit by 160% in my first year.

The success story describes how you did it:

When I became principal of the lower and middle school at Eagle Rock Prep, I inherited a long-established, but rather tired, summer program that averaged 200 participants and earned about $30,000 extra income for the school.

During the regular academic term of my first year at ERP, I redesigned the summer program's academic curriculum from one stream to three, providing separate classes for remedial, academic and gifted students. I also added a performing arts module to the day camp, so students could also enjoy choral music, dance and drama. And I marketed the improved program in the local newspapers and the area's parenting magazine, something that had never been done before.

The result was that the program grew from 200 to 300 students and earned a net profit of $80,000 for the school.

Example #2

- Reduced customer inquiry response time by 15%, which increased the number of customers each representative could handle per day.

Success story #2

The 15% reduction in response time was achieved by developing a simple system to record the customer reference number in the inventory records in chronological sequence by product ordered. Additionally, I suggested that the computer programmers install an interface that would allow the customer service representative to switch from the customer file to the inventory file while working with the client on the phone.

This interface allowed for instant multiple-choice answers to be readily obtained concerning the status of orders, past purchases and current account information.

Example #3

- Arranged local financing of a $22MM foreign acquisition using creative local (foreign) financing for 98% of the equity in the acquired company without parent company guarantees.

Success story #3

At ABC Company, we had an opportunity to acquire a factory in the Philippines, where there are strict local equity requirements in foreign investor deals. I carefully examined the securities laws, the local banking laws and their interior ministry restrictions on foreign ownership. This revealed a lack of continuity in the connective laws between the various authorizers which gave us a great opportunity. I was able to solicit the services of the senior executives with the company plus certain partners in the local law firm to arrange for a local bank to lend us the necessary funds.

The result was a $22MM foreign acquisition with a $440,000 equity input locally financed yet wholly owned by us.

Example #4

- Directed the engineering rationalization of multi-handed components used in the assembly process, resulting in a bottom-line savings of $2.7MM annually.

Success story #4

When I took over the controller position at Widget-Max Company, I investigated areas of potential internal cost savings in the manufacturing and assembly operations. The Engineering Department educated me on component design and rationale.

With my cost accounting background, I discovered an area that could provide us with practical cost savings. When I saw the same basic components being manufactured – one left hand and one right hand for assembly purposes – I asked engineering to look into the practicality of a common component that would serve both left- and right-side assemblies. No one had ever thought of that before. The result was a very slight increase in the component cost but a dramatic reduction of inventory and the associated carrying cost. This was also a major saving to service companies who had to carry our components in the consumer field.

Over a period of four years, inventories were reduced by $12MM, interest was lowered by $900,000 annually, certain expensive production machinery was sold, labor was reduced, and the unit cost of our end product was lowered by 14%. By the end of the fourth year, this rationalization was saving the company $2.7MM annually after tax.

Getting Comfortable in Relating Your Success Stories

Selling oneself is not a natural gift. For many of us, it's difficult to trumpet our successes and speak eloquently about how we achieved them. But doing so makes all the difference.

Relating success stories is a skill anyone can learn and one which is very important to master. To do this, Hand & Associates recommends a form of programmed learning developed by Dr. Michael Williams and others.

Programmed Learning

This method of programmed learning combines four mediums that will maximize the combination of muscle memory and mind memory: writing, reading, speaking and listening.

At least 15 complete cycles in each session are needed to make this method of programming your memory effective. This is different from rote learning. If you follow the instructions, you will not sound like a parrot.

Programmed Learning Sequence

First, write out your success story. Like any piece of writing, each success story should go through a number of drafts written over at least a few days. Remember it should be written to be spoken and not span more than 180 words in length.

When you are ready, locate a quiet place in your home where you can isolate yourself for an hour of uninterrupted learning. You may find this method embarrassing at first, but you will get used to it. Then begin the first of 15 cycles.

Cycle 1:   (1) Read your success story silently.
(2) Then speak/record your text (most computers and cell phones have built-in recorders/players).
(3) Then listen to the recording as it plays back.
(4) Finally, from memory, write the text down again based on what you recall from the original written version.

Cycle 2:   Repeat this cycle: Returning to the original written version, read the story silently. Then read it out loud as you record it. Then listen to the playback. Finally, again write out the story based on the original version.

Cycles 3-15:   Continue to repeat this cycle at least 15 times.

DO NOT record the text once and play it back 15 times. That process will not work. The method is to see the text with your eyes, to speak the text with your mouth, to hear the text with your ears, and to write the text with your hands.

You must repeat the complete cycle at least 15 times. For some people, it may be necessary to repeat the cycle 25 times.

After six or seven cycles, you will find that you can record the text without reading it—that's okay. What it means is that you have now learned the text. Now you must continue to program the message into your preconscious memory.

If you have several stories to learn, use the following daily routine:

Day 1   AM: Program story number 1
           PM: Program story number 2

Day 2   AM: Cycle stories 1 and 2 once only for reinforcement, then program story number 3
           PM: Program story number 4

Day 3   AM: Cycle stories 1 through 4 once each for reinforcement, then program story number 5
           PM: Program story number 6

Day 4   AM: Drop off stories 1 and 2, then cycle stories 3 through 6 for reinforcement. Program story number 7
           PM: Program story number 8

From here on, you can drop off 2 stories each day from the reinforcement recording.

REMEMBER: You must go through the complete cycle every time. Read silently. Speak/record. Playback/listen. Write.

How the Process Works

You are reading the text, developing visual memory. You are speaking into a microphone and developing muscle memory as your mouth and tongue form the words. You are listening to the recording and developing auditory memory. And you are writing the text, developing muscle memory in your hands. These four combine to give you the most effective means of developing long-term preconscious memory.

As you get further into the programmed phase, some of your word usage will change. Unless there is a substantial difference in meaning, let that happen. It's normal. Your memory mechanisms have now taken over and are affording you the most comfortable recall. This also makes your presentation sound spontaneous. Eventually, relating your success story will become like pushing a button. If asked about how you reduced inventory costs at your last position, you mentally push the inventory success story button—and your story pours out! You will be like an accomplished pianist who has mastered and memorized a piece of music. You will be able to tell your story effortlessly and can attend to other matters, like your vocal expression and how your listener is responding to you.

While it doesn't take long to explain what a success story is, or to show how to create one, or to describe how to program one into your memory, the actual writing and memorization of success stories is a big job and can take weeks of work on your part. The benefit, though, is inestimable. If you can confidently and articulately relate success stories which validate your achievement claims, you will be in a position to impress those individuals whom you meet in your job search. Indeed—you will be light years ahead of where you were before you mastered your own success stories.

Where Are We Now in the Job Search?

If we look at the job-finding business as a three-part process, we have now completed the first phase:

1. Preparation
2. Engagement with the world
3. Closing the deal

Next begins the vital task of marketing yourself through networking and searching for job openings. As you begin this next process, you should possess a new level of comfort, as you know who you are professionally and can present your successes confidently. Now that you have something to sell, it is time to go into the world and sell it. The goal is to secure interviews and get an offer of employment.

CHAPTER 5: NETWORKING TECHNIQUES

"You can get everything in life you want if you will just help enough other people get what they want."— Zig Ziglar

In This Chapter:
- ✓ *Networking is the key to finding your next job*
- ✓ *Networking is a lot easier if you see it as a way to serve others*
- ✓ *Networking begins with those you know and moves to others they know*
- ✓ *Networking is only as effective as your preparation*

This is perhaps the most important chapter in this book, since networking is the key to finding your next job, or maybe discovering if your interests point to a completely new field.

In fact, we'll go out on a limb with the claim that a person who networks well hardly needs a book like this one. If you are competent and many people know it, you will never be lacking in opportunities.

This chapter will examine why networking is important, take a look at what it's really about, and identify with whom you should network. The majority of the chapter offers practical ways to network effectively so you can make it an integral part of your life.

Why Network?

Eighty percent of new jobs are found through networking, and 70% of all jobs are never advertised. Aren't those two reasons enough?

Yes, surfing the web for jobs via job sites is very helpful, but such is really no replacement for good, solid networking. Some sites can, indeed, be extraordinarily useful. Careerbuilder.com. Monster.com. Career Builders. Dice. LinkedIn. Indeed.com. All of these job sites can, at the very least, help you gain practice at writing cover letters and presenting your resume. But, again, making phone calls, having conversations over lunch or coffee, joining a Meetup group, and shaking hands are all simple but, nonetheless, priceless forms of human-contact networking.

Besides helping you meet lots of interesting people, providing the chance to form new and even deep friendships, and possibly even assisting you in finding your future spouse, professional networking can also benefit your career.

Benefits of Career Networking

- Discover jobs that aren't posted.
- Connect with potential employers and allies.
- Enlist your contacts to advocate for you and facilitate introductions.
- Promote your knowledge, skills and talents.
- Identify changes and new opportunities in an industry that many be not widely known beyond those who are directly involved.
- Improve your knowledge of the competitive products and services.
- Identify the prevailing salary range in your target industry.
- Enhance ongoing relationships within an industry.

If you are a successful networker you will have many, many contacts out there in the world. What is important is not that you know them but **that they know you** and think of you at the right moment.

What is Networking?

Most of us readily understand the importance of networking. This understanding, however, doesn't mean that we'll find networking easy or natural. The need to present oneself to the marketplace, to peers, to clients, and to potential employers can be daunting. But the cost of not summoning up the energy, skills, and—let's face it—courage to develop your network can be fatal to career growth and lead to much longer periods of unemployment after a job loss.

If we all examine our individual experiences, we realize that we've met people who believe they can sell anything to anybody. But what if you feel like you can't even sell yourself? Consider the following:

- Networking is staying in constant touch with people in a friendly and helpful way.
- A successful networker is one who has an ever-growing circle of acquaintances, colleagues and friends.
- Even though you network because of the benefits you can gain from being in touch with people who can help you, you are also always available to others and are on the lookout for ways you can serve them.
- Thus, a successful networker sincerely wants to help everyone with whom he or she is in contact.

Seen in this light, networking is hardly phony, since sincere friendship and service are both at the heart of it. Remember, you don't need to be charming and outgoing to network. Our **knowledge** and **friendly desire to serve** are precisely what we have to offer others.

It's very hard for many people to ask others for help. It's **not** so hard, however, to offer help to those who can really use it.

With Whom Should I Network?

Since your aim is to help yourself find a new job—or, if you're currently employed, your next job—you want to focus your networking efforts on those who have the potential to assist you to do so.

Begin building your network by identifying people you already know. Ask yourself the following questions:

- Whom do I know well?
- Whom do I know even if only in passing?
- Whom have I met who might remember me?
- Who can provide me information?
- Who can refer me to others?
- Who can help me find a job?
- Who can actually hire me?

You can use the **Networking List** form at the end of this chapter as a simple organizer.

Identifying Contacts

Here are some categories to consider in creating your list:

- Senior executives with whom you have some relationship.
- Peer-level co-workers, past and present.
- Former employers and supervisors.
- Former employees if you have been a manager.
- Other non-peer co-workers, past and present.
- Recruiters, particularly those who have helped you recruit employees or those you have helped.
- Competitors you have met or worked with on industry matters.
- Clients with whom you have developed profitable and amiable relations.
- Trade or professional association officers and co-members.
- Authorities whose seminars, talks, or presentations you have attended.
- Friends, relatives, and present and former neighbors.
- People you see socially, with whom you play sports or other leisure activities, or just see on the golf course.
- Former school/college mates with whom you've stayed in contact.
- Former teachers and professors.
- Members of your place of worship.
- Individuals with whom you've come into casual contact. For example, a person whom you've met on a plane and exchanged business cards.

How to Network?

We all engage in some sort of networking every day, without even thinking about it. When you pick your child up from daycare, you may talk to the teacher and she in turn tells you something about her day. That's networking. Perhaps you talk to the parent of one of your child's friends and tell him or her about something that happened on the weekend. That's networking too. All networking either allows you to gain information from or impart information to others.

Your goal, as stated earlier, is to stay in constant touch with people in a friendly and helpful way in order to benefit them and yourself.

First-Level Networking

In the first phases of your networking, you'll be contacting people you know, people with whom you've had positive contact in the past, and any individuals you feel you can comfortably speak to.

The best way to contact these people is directly, either by telephone or email, with the phone always being a better means of communication.

These are people whom you know are interested in helping you. Just let them know clearly what you're looking for and ask for their aid.

So, what are you looking for? Simple.

- Jobs they may be aware of.
- People they know and whom they can contact on your behalf.
- Any information that might help you.

It is certainly possible that you can be successful finding a job with first-level networking. You could be lucky like Walter was when he finally told someone what he was looking for. Or, you could be lucky enough to come from a well-connected family. But even if you are lucky or well-connected, don't shut off your networking. Otherwise, you could be right back where you started when it's time to seek out your next opportunity.

Second-Level Networking

First-level networking is what you do with people who already know you and who care about you to some degree. Second-level networking, however, refers to those who have no knowledge of you or your family at all.

First, establish a shared interest with new people, based on what you have to offer each other.

How do you establish a mutually beneficial shared interest? You do this by researching the new contact's needs. If someone recommended this new contact to you, you can talk to the recommender to "pick his brain". Or, you may need to do outside research on the individual and his or her corporate needs.

Essentially, you are developing an every-growing database of information on individuals and companies. You're moving from those you know to those **they** know. Think of it as an inverted pyramid in which you grow from a lesser to a greater number of contacts.

Setting Goals For Each Network Contact and Meeting

Whether it happens over the phone or takes place in person, each network meeting requires both remote and immediate preparation. The remote preparation includes things like reading this book, developing the achievement-style resume with your "Who I Am" statement and your achievement bullet-points, as well as writing your success stories and programming them into your memory.

The immediate preparation includes researching the individual and setting a specific goal for the networking meeting itself. This particular process requires reflection that includes understanding your contact's own needs and desires. After all, your new contact agreed to meet with you for some reason. As for your goal, while you are perfectly free to go in a whole new direction depending on what comes up in the conversation, going into the meeting with a goal provides purpose and focus for you.

Some goals or outcomes for network contact meetings include:

- **Eliciting General Referrals for Networking**: Your goal here is to "fish" for the names of individuals who can help you and whom you will then contact on your own. This person can point you in the right direction.

- **Gaining Specific Referrals for Networking:** Your goal here is to get the individual to contact someone on your behalf. It's even better if this individual can set up a meeting with that person for you. This contact then acts as a kind of bridge for you.

- **Getting the Individual to "Keep an Eye Out for Opportunities":** The goal is to get the individual to at least passively or, in general, be on the lookout for opportunities or jobs that may be of interest to you.

- **Assisting the Individual in Fulfilling a Need for Talent or Resources:** The goal is for you to provide information and assistance that helps the individual. You might provide names of people that he or she could recruit, or vendors or consultants that the individual or their company can utilize, or offer knowledge or expertise you possess that can help him or her.

- **Obtaining Industry, Company or Other Information** from an individual to aid you in your future networking: This goal can help you prepare for meetings with individuals or companies by providing an industry or even a corporate overview. This represents a rich source of intelligence for you. This is a "May I pick your brain?" meeting.

- **Indicating Your Availability for Consulting:** The goal here is to make it known that while full employment may be your wish, you are available for short or long-term consulting.

The 30-Second Summary

For your resume, you prepared a two- or three-sentence written "Who I Am" statement to clearly and quickly communicate what you do and your major skills and accomplishments. The "30-Second Summary" is an expanded, verbal version of this statement. It is the core message which you'll communicate to people the first time you meet them, whether it be in person or on the phone. The purpose of the 30-second summary is to get your message across and to spark interest in you within the first minute of contact. Whether it is fair or not, people make judgments about you within seconds of meeting you based on a number of visual and verbal impressions you may unknowingly provide.

This is why first impressions can be last impressions: If your first impression isn't positive, you may never have a chance to make a second one.

The 30-Second summary should:

- Be geared to be spoken, not read.
- Generate interest in you based on your background, skills and abilities.
- Demonstrate your effective communication skills.

Examples of 30-Second Summaries

Harvard Man

I was very fortunate to have gotten both a Bachelors in Finance and an MBA from Harvard. I joined The First Company in its start-up phase right after graduating and have been with them as CFO for 15 years. I developed the basic financial plan and financial systems for the firm. We have achieved funding from VCs, and I play a major role in all aspects of investor relations. I am responsible for seven direct reports and, ultimately, a team of 25. I believe it's important to give back, so I also serve on the executive and legislative affairs committees of the industry's trade association.

Film Editor

I got started in post-production at Lucasfilm where I trained and supported TV and feature film editors on the (then) state of the art EditDroid nonlinear editing system. At Lucasfilm I served as First Assistant Editor on *Radioland*

Murders, one of the earliest feature films to utilize the Avid non-linear editing system. I have continued to stay on the cutting edge of digital post-production. My editing credits include *Beowulf, Terminator Salvation, Star Wars: Episode VII – The Force Awakens, October Sky*, and *Public Enemies*. I also have edited half a dozen low-budget independent features.

At the end of this chapter is the **Writing Your 30-Second Summary** form. After you complete this form, read it out loud. Critique it yourself and ask for input from family and friends in order to improve it. When you get it as interesting and tight as you can, write a "final draft." Then imprint it in your memory using the programmed learning method detailed in Chapter Four. (1) Read your 30-Second summary silently. (2) Then speak/record your text onto the player. (3) Rewind and listen to the recording as it plays back. (4) Finally, write the text down again based on the original written version.

After you have mastered your 30-second summary, don't be afraid to modify it to fit each situation. Finally, note that the 30-second summary communicates who you are, not what you want.

What you want comes next.

Why Are You Looking for a Job?

During a conversation, if you're asked if you're looking for a new position, be prepared to answer.

If you currently have a job, the best answer is some form of, "I've not yet committed to leaving my present job but am open to new opportunities." Then explain what you would look for and why, making sure all the reasons you give are positive, such as a desire for greater responsibility, more opportunity for growth, and so on. The fact that you have a job is in your favor.

If you do not currently have a job, you don't need to go into why you lost your job. Direct the conversation to talk about what you are good at and the type of job you're looking for.

What You Want From This Meeting

Networking includes getting information that will help advance your career. You may have one or more of the following questions for your contact:

- What's happening in their company or the industry in general.

- What companies or individuals might be helpful either for information or a potential position.

- What information in general that they feel might be helpful.

Do not push your resume at someone who does not ask for it. This practice can undo all your work by making the individual with whom you are meeting feel ill-at-ease. The quickest way to make someone want to avoid you is to pressure him to do something he doesn't want to do or something he doesn't have time for. Further, even if you your contact wants to help by passing your resume along, he may find no individual or company which has an immediate interest. You have now made him a bearer of bad news, so he may avoid talking to you.

Making an Impact with Your Contact

We have already discussed setting your goals for the meeting or contact, how to introduce yourself with your 30-Second Summary, being prepared for the "current employment" issue, and the importance of not pressuring your contact. Now you want to do whatever you can to instill in this person a positive impression of yourself and, if possible, a real desire to actively look and even act on your behalf.

Here are some things you can do to optimize your chances:

- **Before the Meeting:** Take the time to review the 30-Second summary, especially the essential points you need to cover in order to attain the goals you have set for the meeting or contact. Also, rehearse until your statement about your current or former job flows easily and appears (and is) both confident and truthful.

- **Ask and Listen:** At the meeting, ask questions and listen carefully to the responses. By your careful, active listening, you let the individual know that his or her comments are important.

- **Focus on the Positives:** In your discussion, be positive about the work you've been doing and the company with which you've been associated. Be positive about the company that the contact works for. Be positive about the industry in general. Do not, however, appear to be out of touch with the realities that face the industry or specific companies. It's okay to use your success stories where relevant.

- **Remember to Give Information:** Find a way, if possible, to be of help to the contact. For example, tell him about people, services and information that may benefit him. Of course, don't violate any confidences when you do this. At an appropriate moment you can also ask, "Is there anything I can do for you?" If your contact says no, you can add, "If there ever is anything I can do for you, don't hesitate one second to contact me."

- **What level of conversation do you want to reach?** Meetings or conversations can go in many directions, from light and surface to deep and personal. It is important that you ask and listen to determine what type of content you should be providing. The other party, not you, should dictate the level.

- **Know When to End the Meeting:** As important as getting information and making an initial good impression are, it is wise to end the meeting in a timely manner. Be careful not to overstay the initial time allotted unless the contact states he or she wants you to stay longer. Ending at the right moment can leave a great impression that you are to the point and that you don't like to waste busy people's time.

- **Follow Up:** It is imperative that, as you close this meeting, you create your next opportunity to converse either in person, by phone or through e-mail. This link to future communication is almost as essential as any other information you might get.

- **Body Language:** As stated earlier, your body language must portray confidence and interest in what the contact is saying. Even if you are on the phone, use the body language you would be using in person. That is, smile, sit forward in your chair and so on.

- **Always Thank Your Contact:** The need to continue and build on the relationship can be fostered by a short, to-the-point letter or email. If possible, provide information that might be helpful to the contact, such as business information, resources, and so on. Also, reinforce your thanks for him or her for taking the time to meet with you.

In the end, it is essential that you be focused, interesting, knowledgeable, and display an appropriate sense of humor. The meeting or conversation must end with some perceived value or satisfaction on the part of the contact. This satisfaction can come from his or her sense of having helped someone, from discovering a new colleague with whom to chat, or from having received information or resources of value.

Networking to Maintain Contact with Personal and Business Contacts

This type of networking is, by far, the most prevalent and often involves lunches or phone conversations with former supervisors, peers and even subordinates, along with former clients, friendly competitors and other professionals from your industry. It is essential that you understand why you are having these meetings and set a specific goal for each of them. One underlying goal that is always present is your desire to maintain your connection with each person.

Online Privacy:

Some people are worried about online piracy. A greater concern for you is online privacy—or the lack thereof.

There is no such thing as online privacy. Everything you post online is "parked" on multiple servers. Any email you write can be forwarded to anyone and everyone.

A good rule of thumb for all online forms of communication—including email—is to never post anything you would not want to see on a huge billboard for everyone to read. In other words, you can never assume that anything you say electronically will remain private. Always be on your best behavior.

Online Networking

The internet offers potentially valuable networking tools. Here we will discuss the most important current ones. We would like to emphasize that even though these are ways of connecting with people, the most important form of networking is direct contact by phone or in person. Thus, online networking is a way to make new contacts which you solidify with personal contact.

LinkedIn

LinkedIn is a social networking site used **specifically** for professional purposes. It can be used to find, meet, and collaborate with qualified professionals.

Much like a digital resume, your LinkedIn profile should display your full name and should be strictly tailored for potential job providers. Your LinkedIn account should list what is on your resume and whatever aboveground, professional, job-related information you know that you'll divulge during the interview process. In other words, there's absolutely no point in talking about your favorite movies, foods and music here. Just keep it straight, simple and solid.

LinkedIn helps you progress through the different levels of networking, allowing you to identify people with whom you might like to be connected.

The site displays the number of people "separating" you from that person. For example, I'm directly connected to Johnny, who knows Mark, who knows Jeff, who knows Josh, who's directly connected to me. So we're three degrees apart. Such is merely one of many networking features that LinkedIn offers.

But in order to maximize your networking effectiveness on LinkedIn, you will need to have your "Who I Am" statement and some highlights from past jobs ready when you create your account. Once you have set up your account and completed your profile, you are now open to a wide network of professionals and posted positions. When you sign in and click on the "Jobs" tab, you'll be able to search for jobs in specific areas worldwide. With a wide range of search options, you can search for people and companies and expand your network in a targeted way.

Twitter

Twitter is a free social networking and micro-blogging service that enables users to send and read other users' updates known as tweets. Tweets are text-based posts of up to 140 characters in length, that users who are "following" you can see.

If you have developed a following, Twitter is a great publicity tool to get your job search message out. This allows people to know what you are doing in your search currently. This also gives you the opportunity to communicate your wisdom – your expertise – a good publicity strategy.

Blogs

A blog is a website, usually maintained by an individual, with regular entries of commentary, descriptions of events, or other material such as graphics or video. Entries are commonly displayed in reverse-chronological order. "Blog" can also be used as a verb, meaning to maintain or add content to a blog. Many blogs provide commentary or news on a particular subject; others function as more personal online diaries. A typical blog combines text, images and links to other blogs, web pages and media related to its topic. Readers are able to comment on the blog, a special interactive feature of such sites.

Blogs enable you to start conversations with colleagues, clients (past or present), or prospects. There is virtually no cost to start one, except, of course, your time. You can be seen as the expert in a specific field of interest or industry.

Chapter 5: Networking Techniques

<u>Facebook</u>

Facebook is a social networking website launched in 2004 with more than 1.44 billion active users per month worldwide, as of September 2015. With Facebook you can reconnect with people with whom you've lost contact— former clients, colleagues, college buddies—as well as keep connected with your current contacts on a regular basis.

Your Facebook profile can be completely open or selectively open to other viewers. You can specify the amount of information you want others to see. Although some people prefer an open profile, we recommend that you always keep your personal Facebook account private to create boundaries between your professional and personal lives.

This more personal account should be strictly accessible by your friends and family—NOT your future boss. At the most superficial level, the NAME of the account should be different from the name on your professional account. It should be more unique, e.g., instead of, say, KevinHand@Facebook.com (which would be a perfect name for my professional account), my personal account might have a less-conventional name like Kevin123@Facebook.com. As many of us who have private Facebook accounts know, it's a most helpful networking system in terms of linking you up with people you've never seen or heard from before or haven't seen or heard from in a long time, such as classmates with whom you may have gone to high school or college—IF, that is, you want to be linked up with them. Let's face it, you may not want to connect with certain individuals from your past. With that idea in mind, another good thing about Facebook is that it gives you the option of very subtly not answering inquiries from possibly undesirable people who wish to join your account or vice versa.

Another excellent reason for separating your professional life from your personal Facebook account is that a lot of private information can be had by an employer or by someone who is going to use it against you. For example, you may post a message on your professional Facebook account stating that you went out on Saturday night with your friends to a nightclub, partied, and got drunk. Those are things that you never include on your professional LinkedIn account and would not want a potential employer to see. Also, you don't want to include an inappropriate or unflattering photo of yourself on your professional LinkedIn account for obvious reasons.

An Important Note Regarding Online Networking

Be careful about spending time on these online networking sites. Each site can potentially engage you full-time. Include time for online networking in your schedule but you do not want to lose sight of the absolute fact that in-person networking yields the best results. Some people can use these online sites to avoid getting out of the house. Use these resources wisely and consider them nothing more than a networking tool.

Networking Group Meetings

Networking groups give people seeking jobs the opportunity to meet others with similar objectives and interests. Often members share job leads. Our advice is to concentrate on one-on-one networking efforts.

Social Events, Professional Association Gatherings, Golfing, etc.

Look at social events, professional association meetings, visits to health clubs, golfing outings and the like as networking opportunities. By meeting people and getting them to talk, you can make new contacts which can lead to passive or active efforts on your behalf.

"Over Exposure"

I vividly recall one example of a young woman who almost got a job with one of our clients—emphasis on the word "almost".

This female candidate included the name of her, supposedly professional Facebook account on her resume when she applied for an accounting position, with the main picture on her account showing her in a skintight, relatively 'revealing' bikini—tattoos, moles, Goosebumps and all exposed. In turn, when several male employees from the accounting department directly involved in the hiring process saw this bikini shot, they immediately got a little overly enthusiastic. In fact, one of the males went so far as to passionately state to a representative from the company's HR department, "Wow! She's probably one of the best-looking accountants we'll ever have!"

With that, HR dropped the young lady like a hot potato. Why?—because Human Resources wasn't going to have that kind of unprofessional attitude amongst employees in the workplace. In fact, the problem had already begun! And it wasn't so much the young lady in the bikini as it was the completely out-of-line reaction from the guys in Accounting, all of whom we learned were later disciplined, quite appropriately, because of their inappropriate behavior. HOWEVER...had that same young female candidate included a photo of her wearing a tasteful dress or executive's suit on her professional Facebook account instead of a drool-inducing bikini, she may very well have landed the job. Remember: Jobs very often are lost on the little things, not the big things. Details—like a simple photo on your Facebook account—will kill you if you don't properly address them.

Meeting Recruiters

Meeting with a successful recruiter is often easier said than done. The reason is that recruiters are busy recruiting the best candidates whom they can find for jobs so that they, the recruiters, can get paid. Any contact with a recruiter is precious. You want to do your best to communicate who you are and try to be helpful. In some industries, a recruiter might contact you to recommend someone for a particular search. If you are the perfect candidate or know a good candidate, this is your "in" to contact the recruiter.

If you help a recruiter once, you can bet that they will ask for your assistance again.

As is often the case in networking, it's not so much who you know as who knows you. If your recruiter friend, for example, is talking to another recruiter, he may say, "I think I have just the person for you." In this way, he is working on your behalf without you even realizing it.

Chapter Six discusses recruiters in greater depth.

<u>Carrying a Business Card</u>

Consider having a business card with your contact information as an important "leave-behind" when you meet someone new. The card can list your specialty and might also indicate your availability as a consultant.

Tracking Your Networking Efforts: Record-Keeping

The networking process can be lengthy and complex when you're busy making new contacts. It is essential to develop a tracking system for the process to make sure you are engaging in a timely and fruitful follow-up.

Likewise, the value of meetings, phone calls, etc., can be wasted if you do not record both obviously important information and seemingly unimportant anecdotal information. The question of what to record can be answered by two questions, one obvious and the other less so: What is important to me? and What is important to my contact? Your contact's relationship with Stephen Spielberg may be very important to you if you're an aspiring film director, but the fact that your contact has a one-year-old daughter named Joannie is important to him.

Imagine what it could mean for this contact if you were to call him after the space of a year and at the end of the call inquire, "By the way, how is Joannie doing? She must be, what, two now?"

At the end of this chapter are two forms that can help you. One is a general **Networking List** form. The other is a more detailed **Planning Networking Phone Calls/Meetings** form to plan the call or meeting and to record the outcomes.

Following Up on a Meeting or Contact

Below is an example of a thank-you letter you could send after a networking meeting. Obviously you should customize your letters. The principle is to underline positive results from the meeting and acknowledge the time and effort that the individual has or will spend on your behalf. (This format is very similar to the one discussed for interview follow up and thank you letters referenced in Chapter 7.)

Dear Sam:

Charles Smith told me that taking the time to meet with you would be very rewarding, and he was absolutely right. Thank you very much for your time and for the referrals that you suggested I contact. It was very helpful to hear your optimism about the current growth of your company.

The information that you have provided has already yielded me two meetings that have been very substantive.

I want to thank you again for your time, the efforts you have extended on my behalf and any suggestions that you might have in the future. I will be having lunch with your CFO, Steve, next week and appreciate the introduction.

Of course, if I can be of help to you in any way, please don't hesitate to contact me.

Sincerely,

Targeting Potential Employers

Identify five to ten companies for whom you'd like to work. Do research to identify the executives at those companies who are in charge of those areas in which you want to work. Then try to determine exactly how you could help each company on your target list. Finally, set about contacting those individuals.

This is a far superior technique compared to approaching the HR department of those companies or just blindly sending out resumes.

<u>Telephone Techniques for Networking and Career Search</u>

The telephone is probably the most powerful tool you have in your career search. Using the telephone effectively can mean the difference between being forgotten to becoming a live candidate. On the hiring side, telephone interviews are popular "first contact" tools for executive recruiters and hiring managers.

Most job seekers resist using the telephone when looking for work. They are uncomfortable calling strangers and fear rejection. In this case, online networking can work against you if you use it to avoid making actual phone calls.

When it is a matter of making calls, the keys to success are researching the company and individual you are calling, determining how you might fulfill a need, rehearsing what you want to say and planning for common blocks you will receive. (Blocks are discussed later in this chapter.) Your preparation will give you a lot of confidence because you'll have something to say and know how to say it.

When it's a matter of receiving calls, the keys are: anticipating various types of calls you may receive, planning what you want to say, and then practicing handling these situations before they occur.

<u>Benefits of Telephone Contact</u>

Here are some benefits to using the telephone to advance your job search.

- **Verified Contact:** A call ensures that you are contacting the right person. A letter and resume may or may not reach the person with hiring authority. By simply making a telephone call, however, you know immediately whether the person has your materials.

- **Immediate Feedback:** You get instant feedback from the telephone. When a company has an opening, you can advance to the next step. If nothing is available, you can move ahead and not waste time waiting for a written reply.

- **Interactive Contact:** During a phone call, you can tailor your presentation to the other person's concerns. You can shift your style to match their expressions of interest. You can also help the contact consider other ways you might fit into the company.

- **Demands Attention:** The telephone has a way of pulling people away from other tasks and activities. A letter or resume may sit in a stack of mail, but a ringing telephone is usually answered immediately. This truth may seem somewhat cold and unfair, but it's still both accurate and thus realistic.

- **Information Calls**: Collecting information about advertised jobs or specific companies is an important part of job hunting. The telephone can be your means of getting this information. Most people are willing to help and can share much that is useful. Be brief, sensitive to the person's workload and appreciative of whatever assistance is provided. This call is also a low-stress one on your part.

- **Calling on Advertised Jobs**: When pursuing advertised jobs, call someone inside the company who knows about the job. You may have to ask around to determine exactly whom it is you should call. Ask about job duties, the key skills required and decide if you "fit" what they want. This information will help you present your skills in a way that meets their needs.

More Telephone Tips

The following tips will increase the effectiveness of networking on the phone. Study them carefully now, then review them before making calls.

Preparing for Calls

Do your homework before making each call. Have your planning notes in front of you during the call. Include the first and last name of the contact, information about the company and key points you want to make. Also, list the outcomes you'd like to achieve such as a face-to-face interview, a referral, answers to questions, agreement to call back or more information about the company.

Timing Your Calls

Time your calls for the best results. Make important calls early in the morning; leave less important ones for later in the day. When calling long distances, remember time zone differences. If it is a long-distance call, mention where you are calling from to receive a higher priority. It is also important to vary the time of day when calling the same individual multiple times. Try early morning, then before lunch, then afternoon and finally after 5:00 p.m.

Communicating with Secretaries and Assistants

Communicating effectively with secretaries and assistants increases your chances of talking to important contacts. Secretaries are often asked to screen calls before putting them through. The way to help them do their job and still talk to the contact is to state your name immediately and then ask for the contact by first and last name. If asked what the call is about, refer to the mutual acquaintance who told you to call, or mention that you are following up on correspondence. In other words, let her know that you have a good reason for calling.

If told your contact is unavailable, ask for a good time to call back. Do not leave your number! When you do, you lose control and have to wait two or three days for a response. If nothing else works, try calling before 8:00 a.m. or after 5:00 p.m. Why these odd hours? It is not unusual to find the top people at a company working before anyone else arrives or after everyone else has gone home. A writer we know wanted to submit a script to Icon, Mel Gibson's production company, through a development executive at that company. Whenever he called, an assistant answered and his messages were never returned. Finally, for the heck of it, he called on a Saturday, and Mr. Gibson himself answered the phone.

Speaking with Contacts

When speaking with anyone at the company you call, sit up straight or stand, speak directly into the phone, smile as you speak, and picture yourself meeting in person. These things add life to your voice.

When you reach your contact, begin by introducing yourself, then refer to your mutual acquaintance or something in your letter or resume. Promise to be brief, present your "30-Second Summary," then wait for a response.

Don't be surprised if you are passed from one person to another during your call. If you are, repeat your pitch to each contact with whom you speak. You may not like repeating yourself, but those contacts you reach are hearing you for the very first time. You want to make as good an impression on each one as you can.

Ask open-ended questions that cannot be answered "yes" or "no." Getting the contact talking is much more important than completing a "canned" presentation. After a period of time, refer to your promise to be brief and offer to end the conversation. Try to reach agreement for continued correspondence, or, ideally, a face-to-face meeting. If you have clearly defined objectives before making each call, you'll have an easier time achieving key results.

Chapter 5: Networking Techniques

<u>Handling Blocks</u>

Sometimes contacts throw out blocks such as, "We're in a hiring freeze," or, "We don't have any positions open right now." When this happens, still try to get something of value from the call. Seek advice on where to go next, ask for a referral, or probe for information about other companies. Notice how the job seeker in the following example effectively handles a block.

Job Seeker: I have over six years of experience supervising the assembly of surgical products. I've worked in both clean-room and non-controlled environments. In addition, I helped with the development of—

Contact: I'm sorry, but we don't have any openings right now.

Job Seeker: I wasn't thinking you'd necessarily have a job for me. My reason for calling was to ask if you know of anyone who might need my skills.

Contact: I can't think of anyone at the moment.

Job Seeker: Well, thanks anyway. Oh, one quick question. Do you know if Johnson & Forster makes their supplies here in town?

Contact: Yeah, their assembly plant is out of Evergreen Street.

Job Seeker: Who's the plant manager?

Contact: I'm not sure… I know I've talked to the guy several times. Oh, yeah, his name is Bill Jacobsen.

Job Seeker: Thank you very much. I'll call him.

Availability is an unusual virtue because it doesn't seem to be on anyone's list, even though it has been around from the beginning.

What is availability like? When you are with an available person, it seems like he or she has all the time in the world for you. The available person also has empathy for you. You feel they really care about you.

In the relationship with an available person, there is often a sense of inequality but *not* inferiority. We seek out a certain person because we need something. We believe that the other person is able to help us. Think of a daughter wanting to talk to her father; a student who goes to his teacher for extra help; or an employee who goes to his boss with a problem.

The person we go to, the one who we see as being able to help us attain something, seems "superior" to us for that reason. When this "superior" person we seek has the virtue of being available, we discover something which is an absolute treasure—this person actually sees value in us. We are treated with the dignity we know deep down we deserve but so seldom receive. We appreciate that this important person listens to us, gives us their time, and understands us.

Even more, not only do we feel listened to and respected, we are actually served. The person with the virtue of availability acts for our good.

Perhaps we don't realize this fact, but we are (or could be) that kind of available person to many. As much as we need and revel in the affirmation of an available person, we need to <u>be</u> the available person to those individuals who treasure us—our spouse if we are married, our children if we are parents, our students if we are teachers, our colleagues if we work outside the home, and any other person who is in need if we can help meet that need.

The WRITING YOUR 30-SECOND SUMMARY Form

WHY THIS?
Given what you want to accomplish with your networking, what is your relevant background and experience?

_____

_____

_____

_____

STRENGTHS
Next, list three or four key strengths which you want to include.

1. _____

   _____

   _____

2. _____

   _____

   _____

3. _____

   _____

   _____

4. _____

   _____

   _____

SUMMARY
Now incorporate the points which you've listed above into the first draft of your summary. Be sure to keep it brief; it should be 30 seconds or less when read.

_____

_____

_____

_____

Practice it out loud. Record it, listen to It, and critique it. Try it out on friends. Revise it. Program it into your memory. Modify it for particular circumstances.

The NETWORKING LIST Form

NAME	TITLE & COMPANY	PHONE	DATE CONTACTED	REFERRED BY

The PLANNING NETWORKING PHONE CALLS/MEETINGS Form
Before the Meeting

PRE-MEETING INFORMATION

Name of Contact: _____

Company: _____

Phone Number/Location: _____

Who Referred: _____

Objectives of Call: 1._____

2._____

3._____

CONVERSATION CONTENT

What will I say to start the conversation?

_____

_____

_____

_____

_____

What are my ideas on how to best approach the contact?

_____

_____

_____

_____

_____

What are my expectations from this meeting?

_____

_____

_____

_____

_____

The PLANNING NETWORKING PHONE CALLS/MEETINGS Form
After the Meeting

POST-MEETING RESULTS

Resume Requested? Y / N   If yes, give to whom?_____

Follow up info (email/phone): _____

Date of Follow-up: _____

Contact Quality:_____

Referrals Provided: 1. _____

2. _____

3. _____

CONVERSATION OVERVIEW

Topics Discussed:

_____

_____

_____

What information can I give them (on me to further conversations, to help them, etc.)?

_____

_____

_____

How can this contact help?

_____

_____

_____

What kind of resource will this person be to me?

_____

_____

_____

Next Steps:

_____

_____

_____

CHAPTER 6: RECRUITERS

"Be so good they can't ignore you."— Steve Martin

In This Chapter:

✓ *Recruiters work for companies, not you, but this doesn't mean they can't help you a great deal*
✓ *Work to get noticed by recruiters but respect their time and interest constraints*
✓ *Be open, honest, and professional during every step of the search process*
✓ *The recruiter's role is to help you secure an interview. You are ultimately responsible for securing the position*

This chapter is about understanding the recruiter and the role that he or she can play in your job search and overall career. In many industries, the recruiter is an important part of your immediate job hunt and a valuable contact as your career progresses over the years. Not only can a recruiter help you find a job now, he or she can also help you obtain better jobs as you grow in your career.

To use this personnel resource effectively, it is important to understand the different types of executive recruiters, their motivations, and the best way to build relationships with them. Successful career management requires that you be able to attract the attention of the search consultant and have the knowledge and skills to use the consultant as a resource and ally in your job search.

Although recruiters can be incredibly helpful in developing your job search, keep in mind that the recruiter's role is to help you secure an interview. Ultimately, the one who is responsible for securing a position is *you.*

The Reasons Companies Hire Search Firms

The type of job you are looking for will determine whether or not a recruiter is important in your individual job search. Not all positions require an outside recruiter. Often, lower-level to middle-management-level jobs are handled by in-house recruiters. The following are some situations when a company hires an outside senior recruiter:

- At the higher senior-officer levels, when the position is crucial to the operations of the company;
- When a position involves a high-demand specialized skill or experience, and where there is a small population with the desired skill set;
- If confidentiality is critical for the search, such as when a company is replacing an employee before the position is vacant;
- When there are political issues that make a neutral third party important to the success of a search;
- To save time and money—sometimes companies do not have enough in-house recruiters or these recruiters are not effective in a certain field; devoting the required time and resources internally for a search would be expensive and extremely inefficient;
- When the hiring authority does not have the expertise to conduct a search from start to finish. For example, the volunteer board members of a non-profit business have to select an executive director but they have no experience in doing so.

Regardless of why companies hire outside recruiters, it is important for you to understand that the recruiter works not for you but for your potential employer. The recruiter is only interested in you to the extent that you can help their client.

Types of Search Firms – Retained vs. Contingency

A company can choose either a retained or a contingency-based recruiter. A retained firm is paid a retainer upfront, whereas a contingency firm is only paid when the employer hires a candidate they have referred. Both firms are paid either a flat fee or about a third of the candidate's first year's compensation.

A retainer arrangement is likely to mean that one recruiter has the exclusive assignment for filling the job, whereas a number of contingency-based firms could be competing to fill the same job. Corporations generally use retained firms to fill jobs to which they attach the most importance.

If a recruiter contacts you about a specific job, an intelligent question you can ask is whether his firm has the exclusive right to present candidates, then you know whether you are one of a select few or part of a cattle call. If a contingency-fee-based recruiter is the exclusive recruiter for a job you want, that is just as good for you as if the recruiter is working on a retainer.

Specialist vs. Generalist, Large vs. Boutique

Specialist search firms know the language of their specialty area, the current trends, and the major players in the industry they serve. The generalist search firms are specialists only in executive recruiting, and are expert in search and candidate-evaluation techniques. They rely primarily on new research for each search assignment.

If you are contacting recruiters—rather than them finding you—a specialist firm will be the best contact for you if one exists for your specialized area. For example, if you are a C.P.A. seeking a senior-level accounting position, recruitment firms exist to fill just these positions.

Another choice a company faces is whether to work with one of the "big name" firms or a smaller firm, often referred to as a boutique firm. The large, well-known firms typically have several offices and extensive resources to draw on, with upwards of 100 employees in each office and groups of specialty areas. Major corporations often retain these well-known firms to fill their top executive positions when they need to have instant credibility or for internal political reasons.

When firms have multiple locations, each office may operate independently or may share search work or databases. The boutique firms range in size from two partners to 20 or more and generally are based in one office.

For your part, if you are recruited by a search firm, knowing whether the company is retained or contingency-based, whether it is a specialist or generalist, or whether it is large or boutique can help you understand something about the prestige of the position or the company that is hiring. On the other hand, if you are contacting recruiters, investing a lot of time developing a relationship with a recruiter in a boutique firm which specializes in just one industry or kind of job can be extremely valuable or a waste of time, depending on your goals.

The Recruiting Process—What to Expect

If you are involved in a job search with a recruiter, it is good for you to understand the typical steps that occur in the recruiting process once a recruiting firm is engaged.

A job specification is written. The recruiter works with the company to develop a detailed job description. This can be four to 10 pages long. While some of the information is key and relevant, some of it may be standard language, put in for presentation purposes. Usually the beginning of each section of the job description will contain the most relevant information. For your part, the job description will be key to how you present yourself in your resume, cover letter, "Who I Am" statement, and success stories, when you present yourself to both the recruiter and anyone at the company. The "mirror" technique can be applied to the entire recruitment process for a particular job in a particular company when you possess such detailed information.

Candidates are identified. The recruiter next develops a list of potential clients. The recruiter or others at his firm may call target companies to contact specific individuals who can become candidates or who can make referrals of potential candidates. A recruiting firm will also often have already-developed lists of contacts. Of course, if you hear of an opening and learn which firm is handling the search, you can call the recruiter, pitch yourself, and submit a resume to try to put yourself into the candidate pool. In keeping with our overall philosophy, we recommend you call the recruiter rather than just submit your transom resume. The call gets you noticed and can yield important information for you.

The recruiter makes calls. If you are called, great! What can you do to get called more often or ever? Remember that some of a recruiter's calls are to get referrals. This is another reason for you to network constantly. The recruiter may not know you, but he might know a senior-level executive who knows you. Or, the recruiter may call Mary Jones to ask her if she would be interested in looking at another position. Mary may say she isn't interested, but she knows of someone highly qualified who might be interested: you!

Develop a Cheat Sheet!

Put your 30-second Summary on an index card, fold it in half and keep it in your wallet or purse. This way, you'll have it with you at all times.

You can get a call from anyone at any time. Be ready.

Resumes are collected and screened. Based on the match between the job specifications and the resumes they receive, the recruiter will decide which candidates he/she wants to interview. This process could take a few days or many months. For example, a job search could be done for a position that will be open a year after it is advertised. If the search seems to be taking a very long time, it may mean that either the recruiter spoke to you very early in the process or that the recruiter has you "on hold." That is, he or the company likes your background but isn't sure if you fit the job qualifications well enough to continue the process. They are probably interviewing other candidates and will make the decision on your candidacy after they evaluate others.

Interviews with the recruiter. The interview with the recruiter is part interview, part audition. He or she will be evaluating your qualifications. At the same time, he or she will be evaluating how well you might "play" in the client's company. At this meeting, you should be active, not passive. A recruiter wants to present individuals to the firm's clients who will be impressive. A candidate who is at the interview just to sit, listen, and judge the opportunity will likely not continue in the process.

One thing to remember when interviewing with a recruiter is not to appear too eager for the position. To get companies to hire them, recruiters have to showcase their expertise to their potential clients. Job searches are not easy—companies need to understand that recruiters often search (literally) the world to uncover just the right candidates and then use their diplomatic and persuasive skills to get these candidates to consent to interviews. This is why transitioning executives—that is, those folks without current jobs and, in turn, are eminently available—are sometimes at a disadvantage with recruiters. A rapidly available executive looks too easy and could lead the company to wonder why they even hired the recruiter to begin with. Recruiters want to avoid this misrepresentation by remaining a bit wary of overeager candidates. However, as long as the candidate shows that he or she is looking at numerous employment options and is only willing to make a move to the right position, he or she should be able to circumvent this issue.

Learn about the position by asking questions of the recruiter, and be realistic about the situation and possibilities. You may decide, after speaking with the recruiter, not to pursue this job despite the fact that you really need a job. At the same time, even though you may wish to continue, the recruiter and the company may not continue to pursue you as a candidate. Console yourself with the idea that this may not have anything to do with your qualifications.

It is also possible that you will not interview with the recruiter. Some recruitment firms simply present an agreed-upon number of qualified candidates to the company, and the company takes it from there.

Finalists meet with client. Although the recruiter will set up these meetings, this is the only part of the process that is just about you and the potential employer. Based on your discussions with the recruiter and your own research, you should be very prepared for the interview, with an understanding not only of the job and the company, but also of the executives with whom you will be meeting. Often a recruiter can give you valuable insights into the executives and the dynamics of the organization. It is in the recruiter's favor for you to look good, since he or she has presented you to their client. The recruiter wants you to do well, so they will usually provide you with any information they have to assist you. Chapters Seven and Eight on interviewing will also assist you in presenting your best case at your company interview.

Education is verified and references are called. Recruiters will confirm that you have received the degrees you have listed on your resume. They often require a date of birth or Social Security Number to gather this information.

The recruiter, or people from the company hiring, usually check a minimum of three references, and often call at least one supervisor, peer, and one subordinate. The number of people and whom they call will depend on the position requirements and any concerns they may have about your qualifications. By the time you are offered an interview with the company, you should have put together a list of references. On your list, include the highest quality, most articulate persons you can recruit on your behalf. Make sure these references enthusiastically support you. It is also essential to let your references know that they will be getting a call from a recruiter. Giving them an understanding of the position and its requirements will also help their discussion with a recruiter. It is a good sign to a recruiter if your references are very responsive and enthusiastically and articulately promote you. On the other hand, if you references do not return calls or are not eager to discuss you, the recruiter will rightly interpret their behavior as a negative reflection on you.

An offer is made and the negotiating process begins. A point will be reached when the employer would like to hire you and make an offer. The success of your negotiation will depend to some extent on your mastery of the dynamics of a bargaining situation conducted through a third party— the recruiter. Make sure you are up front about all aspects of your previous compensation package. This should include not only base and bonus, but also equity, car allowances, vacation, and any other cash and benefits. Let the recruiter know what you expect. Recruiters don't like surprises as they may look foolish in front of their clients.

The recruiter will also try to prevent the client from looking foolish in front of you. Often a recruiter can stop a company from giving a candidate a very low offer that will hurt the bargaining process. The recruiter's job at this point is usually to do whatever it takes to get you in that job. He or she can often be a big ally of yours at this stage if you know what you want and are reasonable. At the beginning of the process, you are selling yourself to the company, however at this stage the company is selling themselves to you, and the recruiter is the matchmaker.

For an in-depth discussion of job offer negotiation, see Chapter Nine.

Ongoing relationship with the recruiter. If you are hired, you will likely hear from the recruiter throughout the first year in your new position. There are a number of reasons for this:

- You are a success story. The recruitment firm thinks positively of you and feels a strong rapport. They genuinely want to know how you're doing in your new role.
- Most recruiters have a 12-month guarantee with their client company. Thus, if you leave within the first year, they must redo the search at no charge. For this reason, it is very important to them that you are happy.
- You may be an excellent resource to them for future searches.
- You may be a source of new business for them.

On your part, whether you are successful in finding a position or not, you have created an ally who can help you in the future.

Getting Noticed By a Recruiter

This section discusses ways to increase the probability that recruiters will find your name for appropriate searches.

Contact the Recruiter

Sending resumes to recruiters should be a key part of any job seeker's plan. However, the recruiter works not for you but for the client and only has a limited number of searches at one time. Thus, most of the time recruiters will only be able to assist you if your background matches the requirements for one of their searches. That is why you should send your resume out to a number of recruiting firms.

Since you are looking for work, this is the time to reconnect with every recruiter who has assisted you or you have assisted in the past. If they know you and you call, they'll often take the time to tell you whether there are searches going on in their firm which could fit your background. Large firms may have many hundreds of searches in progress. The recruiter may even be able to provide job leads for positions his firm is not representing.

Network, Network, Network

Networking is the most valuable way to be noticed by a recruiter. Keep in contact with employees from your previous company and, if it is not too cost prohibitive, join associations that are relevant for your industry. Let everyone know you are seeking work. The more people that can refer you to recruiters, the better. Also utilize your alumni network. Make sure to contact any recruiter who is an alumnus from your college or graduate school.

Get Published

Another good way to bring yourself to the attention of your colleagues, your industry and executive-search professionals is to write an interesting article. Your focus should be getting an article into a trade magazine or on a trade website. Trade journals for specific industries are always looking for fresh material. Their editors are especially open to contributions from people who can provide something different and interesting. Don't overlook alumni magazines, LinkedIn posts, and blogs.

Use Search-Firm Websites

Search firms are increasingly posting jobs on their websites. As long as you know that the search firm is reputable, you should apply for any appropriate jobs. Some companies allow you to enter your resume into their database, so your name may come up even if you're not aware of a specific job. For one example, see Korn/Ferry's Futurestep.

If a Recruiter Calls You

If a recruiter calls you, note the name of the recruiter and the company. If you are not familiar with the firm, you may want to ask what kind of firm they are: retained, contingency-based, large, boutique, etc. Be sure, also, to ask how the company heard of you; this provides you real-world feedback on the success of your networking efforts.

As discussed, contingency firms are paid only if a candidate they present is hired. They are often looking for as many candidates as possible to present to their clients. In contrast, the retained firm serves as an exclusive consultant to corporate management and, like an attorney or CPA, has its fees and expenses paid by the client, whether or not a candidate is chosen.

At this point, the recruiter's goal is to present the opportunity. If the job is one you are interested in, say so and ask what you should do next. If the proposed opening is not appropriate for you, it's still in your best interest to welcome the caller and handle his or her questions and requests in a courteous, business-like manner. Your professional response will be remembered and the recruiter could be a strong ally in your career development.

Don't worry about hurting your relationship with the recruiter if you are not interested in the job. Be sure to offer the recruiter referrals if you have any. You can even say something like, "I can't think of anyone to refer to you off the top of my head, but if you like, I could think about it and call you back." Solid, viable recommendations that make sense to the recruiter reflect well on you. However, do not pretend to have an interest in the job just to build a relationship with a recruiter. This will waste the recruiter's time and therefore have the opposite effect.

Once you have done something for the recruiter by offering referrals, thank the recruiter and say you appreciate consideration as other opportunities arise. Ask the recruiter if there are other positions the firm is handling that might be more in your line. Also, if the recruiter seem open to it, attempt to brainstorm about other search firms and companies that may be appropriate for you. Not all recruiters will be willing to take the time to do this with you. Some may, however, and it is truly worth the effort.

Be Accurate

While a specific degree or an enviable record of accomplishment is not necessarily a requirement of every position, integrity always is. Make sure all materials and conversations accurately reflect your capabilities and track record. Your references and credentials will be checked thoroughly. Anything less than what you have represented destroys your credibility with the recruiter—and you will not be called again.

Casual Martin

Martin was a bright young man who came to me for career advice. He had a referral from someone I knew and respected. But martin was dressed in khakis, a T-shirt with a logo and loafers with no socks. I'm sure if he thought he was going to a job interview, he would have dressed better. Even though he knew I'm a recruiter, he didn't realize that he was interviewing with me also.

When you are looking for a job, when are you formally "on"?

A young friend living in Los Angeles wants to break into Hollywood as an actor. He doesn't close shave every day because he is cultivating that two-day-old-beard look that is currently popular, but he is careful to keep the stubble at the proper length. He never lets his hair get too long or be dirty, even though he carefully grooms it so it looks like he's just gotten out of bed. He dresses as an aspiring actor at all times—even buying clothes that come with artistic rips and holes, as is the style. And he speaks and acts appropriately at all times, in this case, always politely. He lets everyone he meets know his objective—to be an actor—because in a place like LA, one never knows who is a producer, a director, a talent agent, or who knows someone who is.

When you are building your career, you are always interviewing. You are interviewing with every person you meet. This means you are appropriately dressed wherever you go and well-spoken with every person you meet.

My actor friend is always interviewing. And so should you, whatever your career aspirations.

Chapter 6: Recruiters

Remain Professional

Once you have begun discussions in earnest with the recruiter, bear in mind that he or she is not your therapist, counselor, or cleric. Confessions, ethnic jokes, over-familiarity, and gossip are not appropriate in any of your dealings with a recruiter. When meeting the recruiter at his or her office, treat everyone you meet with warmth and courtesy. This is both human decency and good business practice because even the receptionist may be asked for an opinion of your presentation and conduct.

Also, remember that a recruiter is retained by the client company to serve as its—not your—representative. You should, therefore, treat the recruiter just as you would the potential employer in all your contacts. More than one candidate has shown up in casual attire for a recruiter meeting and lived to regret it.

Know Your Constraints

Before the preliminary meeting with the recruiter, have a clear grasp of your own requirements and constraints. You should know your desired level of autonomy, the responsibilities you seek, the compensation you require (and desire) and any pertinent family issues. A child who needs unique medical care or a partner with deep ties to a community may make relocation a deal breaker. Know your non-negotiable terms. These are all factors you took into consideration when you dreamed up your ideal job in Chapter One. Bring these constraints up with the recruiter soon after the process begins. The recruiter will appreciate your forthright evaluation of the situation and work within those parameters for the next opportunity.

A seasoned recruiter will always be able to provide details on job specifications and corporate culture. Gather as much ancillary information about the company as possible and analyze its prospects, products and services, place in the industry, growth plans and management team. Evaluate the position's responsibilities, reporting path and personal growth potential. Ask yourself: "How do I fit into this company? Does the company and position provide for meaningful growth? What are my prospects for promotion? How will this position advance my career?"

Even though a proposed job seems enticing and gratifying, take a moment to critically evaluate the company and the specific position. Comparing this new opportunity to your ideal job. On the other hand, there is nothing wrong with taking a non-ideal job as long as you do so with your eyes wide open.

Too often, candidates are seduced by the opportunity, only to drop out late in the interview process when they fully realize the implications of a job change. By this time an executive recruiter and his or her client will have put a great deal of time, effort, and even money into your candidacy and will be frustrated if you pull back after several interviews. If at all possible, evaluate what you are getting into before becoming too deeply involved.

Interact Directly with the Recruiter

Do not bypass the recruiter by submitting resumes directly to the company. The company will only forward them to the recruiting firm, and they might get lost.

Once you're involved in a series of company interviews, direct your communications with the company, to the recruiter unless you are told otherwise. In the event that the company calls you directly, keep the recruiter informed.

Finally, don't hesitate to send a note of appreciation to the recruiter. Whether an offer is made to you or not, whether you accept or decline a position, a thank-you letter is a class act—and it's memorable.

CHAPTER 7: INTERVIEW TECHNIQUES

"We're supposed to be perfect our first day on the job and then show constant improvement."— Ed Vargo, MLB Umpire

In This Chapter:

✓ *Effective interviews require intensive preparation and rapid follow-up*

✓ *Assume that everyone you encounter in the company is interviewing you, so be professional at all times*

✓ *There are different forms the interview can take, but your objectives are always to learn what you need to know about the position and to communicate how you can fit the company's needs*

✓ *Listen carefully and think before responding to questions. Don't talk for more than two minutes on any one question*

✓ *Match every company need with one of your success stories*

✓ *Be unfailingly positive*

The interview is the heart of your job search because interviews can result in job offers.

Your networking and resume have gotten you an interview. Your success stories have given you the ability to communicate what you have done well and how you have done it. But an effective interview requires further preparation.

This chapter and the next will guide you through the process involved in achieving a successful interview. Chapter Seven is divided into three parts: what to do before, during, and after the interview. Chapter Eight then presents 64 questions that could come up in the interview itself and how to answer each one most effectively for you.

Before the Interview

You have already done a great deal of preparation for your successful interview. You have taken inventory and created your achievement-style resume with its "Who I Am" statement and achievement bullet points. You've carefully prepared a number of "Success Stories" and used them, along with your 30-second summary, in your networking activities. You've done research on your target industries, the company, and the job.

It is recommended that you keep track of contacts you make during the search process; this means that you log all calls to and from each company. When a call comes in for an interview, your log should include:

- Company name
- Date and time of initial contact
- Who called and his or her title
- Date, time and location of the interview
- Who will interview you
- A cell phone number to call in case there are any problems on the day of the interview
- Name of the decision-maker (if known)

To record this information in a convenient form, use the first page of the **Pre-Interview Planning** form found at the end of this chapter.

Preparing for the Interview

When you do get an interview, it is time to launch into your immediate preparation.

- Conduct further research on the company to better understand the key needs of the position you are seeking to fill.
- Apply this knowledge to yourself, tailoring your presentation appropriately.
- Go through the information in this chapter and the next, applying it to who you are in the context of this interview.

- Do everything you need to do to show up at the interview on time, looking and feeling your best.

Company Research

The areas that you should examine include company history, reputation, names of key executives, and, most importantly, what the company does (its services) or manufactures (its products). It can also be very helpful to know the names of the executives who might influence the hiring decision. Check for recent press releases that could indicate financial problems such as threatened mergers, pending layoffs, proposed downsizing, recent sales of company-owned businesses, loss of any major contracts, and any pending product liability legal actions. Also, check for employee lawsuits against the company. There are several websites that report such lawsuits, as well as employee gripes about the company. Glassdoor.com for example, can provide key insight on a company's corporate culture since management cannot hide or alter reviews. Watch for recent executive turnover, particularly those who were with the company less than a year. Such behavior within a company could indicate a changing corporate culture, and you need to understand the emerging way of operating.

On the positive side, look for recent major contracts that the company may have received, as well as community service or other awards. Employee newsletters and employee award and recognition programs are usually an indication of an employee-oriented company.

Personal Presentation Rehearsal

Plan in advance how you'll explain how your competencies and experience match the needs of the organization and the position for which you're interviewing. Tailor your personal presentation and potential responses, selecting demonstrated competencies and success stories which address the needs you've identified.

Rehearse your personal presentation on video if possible.

Day of Interview Checklist:

- Always look professional for an interview
- Be sure that you know where the interview is, how to get there, and where to park
- Memorize the name of the person with whom you will be interviewing
- Always carry a couple of extra copies of your resume to the interview
- Have with you a typed list of at least five references (separate from the resume)

During the Interview

Job interviews are normally conducted by the person who has the authority to hire you or to whom you would report. Sometimes you must pass through one or more screening interviews until you reach the person with hiring authority. Whether the interview is for a newly created or long-established position, the interviewer's job is to determine if your qualifications and experience are relevant to the position and if you are a good fit for this department, division, and the company as a whole. For your part, you also have to make an initial determination of whether the position aligns with your career and personal objectives and if the culture of the department, division, and company is a fit for you.

When you go into your interview, consider this important caveat. Even though you have provided a carefully prepared resume, never assume your interviewer is as prepared as you are or that he has even had time to read it. Your interviewer may know or remember nothing about you. This may be difficult for people who don't like to repeat themselves, but it is essential. Your interviewer may only learn what you tell him in the interview.

Here we will briefly discuss the various types of interviews which you may experience.

<u>The Competency-Based Interview</u>

In the most common type of interview, the interviewer asks you a series of questions based on the job description and the most important needs of the company. An interview like this is designed to find out if you know and can do what the company needs. It tries to uncover whether you are competent to do the job.

Chapter 7: Interview Techniques

By following the advice in this chapter and mastering the questions presented in the next, you will be at a great advantage in a competency-based interview.

The Behavior-Based Interview

The purpose of the behavior-based interview is to find out how you might behave in a given situation or environment. Some interviewers use it throughout the interview, while others only employ it for specific blocks of questions.

For example, if you have applied for a job as a customer service representative, a typical behavior-based question might be as follows:

What do you enjoy most in your work?

Ideal answers in order of importance are:

- I enjoy interacting and working with people.
- I enjoy solving problems.
- I enjoy meeting new people either in-person or over the telephone.

These are good answers because they are specifically relevant to the work that customer service reps do: They work with people to solve problems which have arisen in connection with the product.

The Conversation or Discussion-Based Interview

The interviewer who engages in conversation or discussion will often make long statements and ask for you to respond, or he or she may say a few words and seek to have you ask questions and talk about yourself.

The challenge on your part is to keep a conversational, informal tone yet to communicate why you are the right person for the job. In other words, you may have to direct the interview so that the interviewer learns what you need him to learn.

One of the pitfalls of a discussion-type interview is that you may let your guard down and become too familiar. In that case, you might easily say something which you didn't mean to and, in the process, shoot yourself in the foot.

The Proposal Interview

This type of interview is basically a meeting initiated and conducted by you with a person who has the authority to hire you, or to whom you would report. In preparation for such an interview, you should have researched the firm and identified areas where: (1) its needs and your competencies match, or (2) how you can help the company or division or department solve its problems, or (3) how you can contribute to its success. The structure of the proposal interview consists of your personal presentation followed by questions and answers.

The goal here, as in the straight job interview, is to "close the sale"—something rare in a first meeting—or at least to set up another meeting to continue the exchange of information, perhaps including others at the company.

Interview Performance Tips

Having the ability to get along with people may be the single-most important ingredient for success in business.

Likable people:

- Smile
- Speak in a friendly tone of voice with an appropriate sense of humor
- Ask questions
- Listen
- Use the other person's name

On the other hand, a person is generally disliked if they appear as a braggart or know-it-all, insist on constantly upstaging others with bigger and better stories, frequently swear or use profanity, speak down to others, demand attention, or voices extreme political or religious beliefs.

To come across in a positive manner, act professionally and confine what you say to what is strictly relevant to the job, ask appropriate questions, and listen carefully to the answers. Doing so will practically guarantee your likability since it demonstrates that you value the other person as an authority and makes a person feel sincerely listened to.

Body Language and Facial Expressions

Things to AVOID:

- Wandering eyes: staring out the window, looking at the ceiling or the floor.

- Intense or extreme facial expressions in response to a question. This is why video is your friend. You may be doing this without being aware of it.
- Slouching in the chair.
- Fumbling or fiddling hands or thumbs.
- Putting your fingers in your mouth or generally touching your face. Some body-language experts say that touching your face indicates you are not telling the truth, something people unconsciously pick up on.
- Scratching.
- For men, removing your suit jacket. Never remove a jacket unless the interviewer has. In most cases, it is preferable to decline an invitation to do so.
- Saying yes to invitations for coffee, soda, or water. Such invitations are usually extended as a matter of courtesy, but often pose a nuisance when accepted.

Things to DO:

- Shake hands firmly but not vigorously. A woman should always offer her hand first in any meeting situation. Both men and women should make sure that their hands are not wet or clammy from perspiration.
- Smile frequently.
- If feelings of anxiety begin to arise, take a deep breath through the nose and release it slowly through the mouth, repeating if necessary.

Proper Dress

Appearances are critical to first impressions. Often times a first impression is made before one word is ever spoken. Interviews are a perfect time to 'dress to impress'; be formal and professional, maintaining a meticulously polished look.

- Both men and women should wear conservative colors such as mid- to dark-blues, grays, browns, or black.
- Men should always wear a collared shirt and a conservative tie.
- Shoes must be clean.
- Women should avoid revealing necklines and skirts that are too short. Preference is for the tailored two-piece suit or carefully coordinated separates.

- Both men and women should minimize the use of jewelry. For men, a watch and ring are maximum. For women, conservative earrings, a watch, limited rings and a conservative necklace.
- Hair should be neat and groomed conservatively.
- For men, the clean-shaven look is more desirable for interviewing; for women, conservative makeup.
- Tattoos: If you have them, *cover them*. Once you've proven to your employer that you're a hardworking, competent, valued worker, he or she probably may not care. But you never know. Be safe rather than sorry.

Appropriate Conversation

Many candidates make fatal errors as soon they enter the interview room or just as they are about to leave. The reason is that these are typically less formal moments in any conversation. The fact is that, during every moment you are in the presence of anyone from the interviewing company or their search firm, you are under inspection. Attempts to be funny or ingratiate yourself can easily backfire.

We, therefore, suggest that you:

1. Not tell jokes.
2. Never volunteer religious preferences.
3. Avoid comments about politics.
4. Avoid taking firm positions on current affairs.
5. Avoid discussions about ethnic issues.

Candidates have no way of knowing the preferences of the interviewer, and some skilled interviewers will set up oral traps for candidates, particularly in current affairs.

Skype Interviewing: Recommendations

Employers may wish to first make visual/aural contact with you over a computer screen via a Skype interview. As with any interview, you need to be diligent with your appearance when you participate in Skype interviews. However, you must also consider other details: from visual framing to lighting to background noises, remember that you're judged on presentation and appearance. Is there enough light on your face? Will the dog bark during the interview? We recommend practicing with a friend before you interview on Skype (and in general!). Make sure your surroundings and overall color are to your advantage. Dress as if you are meeting in person.

Men, wear a suit and tie, not just the top part. Women, style your hair and apply make-up. Look in the camera, not the monitor. Smile.

Home Un-Improvement

One Skype interview burnt into our brain was one conducted with a gentleman, Brad, in his early forties while he was in a poorly lit basement and wearing a plaid wool shirt. Not only was the candidate dressed in a totally inappropriate manner for the job interview, but there was an—almost expected but far from desirous—echo in the basement, which, in itself, was somewhat dark and, to be perfectly frank, rather ominous.

Additionally, we couldn't help but notice that hanging on the flat, hard concrete wall behind Brad, were a selection of power tools, ranging from power drill to handsaw to chainsaw. Combine the dark, echoing environment with the impersonal concrete wall, the over-the-top presence of the power tools, and Brad's inappropriate plaid shirt and, well, you can imagine our impression. We thought we were interviewing a cast member of "Home Improvement" or, worse, the latest installment of the Texas Chainsaw Massacre saga!

Again, when interviewing via Skype, always remember your environment and manner of dress:

Make them work to your benefit, not against it.

Your Agenda: What You Want to Accomplish

As you prepared for the interview, your objectives included: (1) collecting information you need to decide if the position is a good fit, and (2) organizing the information to present to the interviewer and convince them that you are the right person for the position. This preparation helps ensure a shared, productive interchange.

Below are some questions you will want answered by the end of the interview. If you have prepared well and the company has done a good job with the materials provided to its candidates, you should know the answers to many of these questions already.

1. **To Whom Am I Speaking**

Get the interviewer's full name and title. This is very basic but important. Try to establish the interviewer's role in the company and his or her relationship to the position you are interviewing for.

2. **What Is the Purpose of the Interview?**

Is this a get-acquainted meeting, a preliminary screening interview, a finalist interview or a second-opinion interview with the hiring manager's superior, your potential peers or the workers who will report to you? Is a hiring decision distant or imminent?

3. **How Much Time Do We Have?**

Determine the time frame. Get an idea of how long the interview will take and what is on the interviewer's agenda. If you know how your time is coming to an end, you may actually need to gently direct the meeting to get across what you think is essential.

4. **What Are the Realities of the Position?**

This area includes many possible questions, including:
- Is this a new or an existing position?
- How long has it been in existence?
- What are the responsibilities and priorities?
- What are the objectives?
- What is the extent of the authority?
- To whom will I report and what is his or her position?
- Where does this position fit in the structure of the company, division and department?
- What is the political constituency for this position? Will I be alone without allies and supporters?
- What criteria will be used to measure success in this job?
- How and by whom will my performance be evaluated?

- What are the financial, physical, and personnel resources available to do the job?
- What is the budget and what will the spending authority be?
- How does the financial and strategic planning process work?
- Has the budget been increased or decreased in recent years?
- What are the reporting relationships?
- Who are the people with whom I will work?
- Do the individuals with whom I would work report to my superior?
- How long has the position been open?
- Who had the position last?
- Why was the person replaced? What happened to that person?
- What might my future look like from a career-track standpoint, including potential promotions, moves or opportunities?

As stated above, your second goal is to show the potential employer that you are the person he or she should hire, and you can do this best by matching your competencies to the needs of the position. Ideally, for each company need, you provide one success story of how you filled just that need for someone else. Thus, you demonstrate that you not only know the right things to say—which is important—but that you have already put these principles into action—something really impressive.

If the person interviewing you is good at what they are doing, both objectives will be fulfilled, as the hiring manager will fully inform you about the company, its culture and the demands of the job, and will ask you questions which will give you an opportunity to connect your knowledge, skills, and successes to the job description.

"How Am I Doing?"

As you sense the interview is drawing to a close, ask for an assessment of how well you match the requirements of the position and the organization. This is an opportunity to bring to the surface questions or doubts that might only come up after you are gone. By asking this question, you may learn where you stand and also gain an opportunity to add more or clarify a point.

The Interviewer's Agenda

Some interviewers are highly skilled, while others have no formal training in interviewing. Some are clearer about what they **don't** want in an employee, but less clear about what they actually need.

The structure and content of employment interviews will change with the skills and goals of the individual interviewers. Some interviews will begin by giving an overview of the company and a description of the position, followed by questions and answers. Other interviewers might reverse the process, eliciting information from you first. Still others might integrate the information-giving and information-receiving components.

Regardless of the experience-level or the interviewing style, there are basic agenda items that an interviewer will need to cover. Having an awareness of what a potential employer needs to know might help you ensure a successful interview. If your interviewer is not effective, you need to gently lead them so that they learn what you want them to learn about you, your qualifications, and your fit for this position.

Most likely, he or she will be seeking information in four general areas.

Competency: You are able to effectively perform the specific job functions.

Behavior: You will respond and behave appropriately in most situations.

Acceptability: You are acceptable both socially and professionally.

Compatibility: You have the required interpersonal qualities to "fit in."

Some Basic Questions the Interviewer Will Likely Have

- Does the candidate have the qualifications and experience needed for the job?

- Does the candidate appear to have the necessary behavioral qualities?

- Does the candidate have any extras or pluses that will benefit us now or in the future? Is this someone we might be able to transfer or promote?

- Does the candidate 'fit' into the organization? Are there any visible flaws in character or style which will inhibit cooperation with peers and subordinates? Is the candidate 'one of us'?

- What are the personal qualities of the candidate?

- How will the candidate's good qualities contribute to the job to be done and to the organization generally? What about the bad ones? Are any series enough to eliminate this candidate?

Additionally, the interviewer will evaluate you on factors like:

Ability to communicate	Maturity
Attitude	Motivation
General intelligence	Self-assurance
Interpersonal relationships	Stability

Deals Over Meals:

If you have a lunch or dinner interview at a nice restaurant, this is not your chance for a free gourmet feast. Don't order whatever you like off the menu. Unless it is against your religion, order what your interviewer orders. If your tastes are like the interviewer, the interviewer is liable to like you, and that counts for a lot. If she orders a steak and you're a vegetarian, okay, order the soy-stuffed portabella mushrooms but don't announce that you find it unethical to eat meat! In the same way, if she orders a drink, order the same one. If you don't drink, don't say you don't drink. Order the drink and just sip it. (Of course, if you are a recovering alcoholic, order a soft drink, without making a big deal out of it.)

The meal interview is not about you: It is about what the interviewer wants. And don't expect to eat much of what you order! You'll probably be too busy talking, and you certainly don't want to speak with food in your mouth. Again, it's not about eating!

Get the job and then go out and order what you want and enjoy every bite of it.

Carla's Surprise

Back in the '80s, Carla had gotten a BA in art, and found that she couldn't find gainful employment in that field. Eventually, she decided to go back to school to get a Master's in marketing, because it was more commercial but still let her draw on her artistic talents. Carla moved back in with her parents—something she didn't at all want to do but felt forced to for financial reasons. Carla knew of a fairly new publisher whose mission she deeply identified with. Through a family connection, she was able to get an interview with the firm. She dressed for success, brought her portfolio, made the half-hour drive to the publishing house's office (a converted home), and met the editor. Carla had a long and positive interview with her. She even met the publisher, a person she had admired for a long time and he 'welcomed' her to their team. She got the job! Only then did she find out what kind of salary the company could offer her. To her chagrin, it was a pittance, not enough to pay the rent on a studio apartment. The interview went sour at that point and Carla couldn't help showing her anger and frustration. When she got back to her car, Carla dissolved into tears.

What mistake did Carla make? Carla had let herself be surprised. She fell in love with the job before she knew if she could actually take it. She hadn't done her research to find out what kind of compensation she could expect from a new, small, non-profit publishing house. If she had found out this crucial information before the interview, Carla could have made a more rational decision. Maybe she could have continued living with her parents for a few more years—made the personal sacrifice in order to do this very meaningful work. In retrospect, she ended up living with them anyway—since it took quite a long time to find her first 'real' job. She thought about that failed interview from time to time as the years passed, and the company grew from having published only 20-something titles to thousands.

"Three Ps" and a Good Fit

How do you show your potential employer that you are a good 'fit' if you've never been part of this company's culture? We believe that the interviewer really wants to know that you will fulfill what is called the "Three Ps". You will not bring problems with you, and you will not cause once you are there. Instead, you will solve problems for the company. Your responsibility is to show the interviewer that you will do the following for their company:

1. **Bring No Problems**

   This means:

   - I am not burnt out.

   - I am not crippled by the circumstances surrounding the departure from my last position.

   - I have not been litigious with former employers, nor caused them to be sued or have regulatory actions brought against them.

2. **Create No Problems**

   This means:

   - I will not make changes without including those who should have a say.

   - I will not make change for change's sake.

   - I will not adopt "shoot from the hip" solutions but instead will demonstrate evaluative processes that seek cost-effective and justifiable solutions to real problems.

3. **Solve Problems**

   This means:

   - I meet the requirements you have identified for the position.
   - My experience and expertise will add value to your company.
   - I will help improve operation and productivity.
   - I know my temperament fits with the organization…
     - …as you have outlined the company culture and style, and/or
     - …as I have witnessed through observation and interaction in the interview process, and/or
     - …through meeting employees, and/or

- ...through prior networking with members of your organization, and/or
- ...through the reputation that your company enjoys.

Understanding How to Answer an Interviewer's Questions

A good interview is a mutual getting-acquainted process with questions and answers flowing in both directions. Some of the questions you will be asked are predictable. Some are very difficult to answer. Chapter Eight will present 64 possible interview questions. You should become very familiar with answering every one of them in terms of who you are. But, in general, follow this template in answering interview questions.

1. **Listen to the question.** Be sure that you understand what is asked and why the interviewer wants this information. If necessary, ask for clarification on the specific point the interviewer is pursuing.

2. **Take time to think** about the question before you respond. Some questions can be answered immediately; others require a few seconds thought.

3. **Give concise answers.** Give enough of an answer to satisfy the interviewer, but don't ramble or volunteer more information unless it is positive and pertinent. Try to keep each response time to less than two minutes.

4. **Be positive.** Always be truthful, but do not offer negative or critical information about a company or an event. Use positive action verbs in the beginning of your answers, such as:

   - "I solved ..."
   - "I developed ..."
   - "As a team leader, I directed ..."
   - "I increased sales ..."
   - "I prepared ..."

This should be second-nature to you, since in all your preparation up till now—in your resume planning, resume writing, 'Who-I-Am' statement, success stories, 30-Second summary and so on, you have done just this.

As bears repeating, if your interviewer is not effective, you need to lead him so that he learns what you want him to learn about you and your qualifications and fit for this position.

The End of the Interview: What are the Next Steps?

Identify the next stage in the selection process:

- When are you likely to hear from the interviewer?
- When should you call if you do not hear from the company?
- What else do you need to know or to do?

After the Interview

During the interview, you might make a few, brief notes. As soon as you can after the interview, however, record everything you can remember on the following subjects:

- The position – are there any previously unstated duties or responsibilities or priorities you discovered?
- The person – indications of what he or she is looking for.
- The company – goals, outlook, philosophy and other relevant issues.
- The cast of characters—who were they and what were your reactions to them?
- The material (answers) you presented – what did you tell them?
- The information you got – what clues did you pick up?
- Did the interviewer dwell on any one subject, or did he or she come back and ask a particular question more than once? This is very important to note because it is either critical to the position or because the interviewer may have a doubt about you in this regard.

Fill out the **Post-Interview Review** form to capture this and other important information.

Write a Follow-Up Letter

Within a day or two, follow-up with a letter to each person with whom you met regardless of how you think the interview went. The letter should be reasonably brief and relevant. Be sure to:

- **Express your appreciation for the time and opportunity**. Avoid hackneyed opening sentences such as: "Thank you for your time." A preferred opening sentence would be: "I enjoyed meeting with you yesterday and having the opportunity to learn more about your company."

- **Emphasize salient points covered in the interview**. If the interviewer repeated a key issue about the job or company, you should mention that point in a positive manner.

- **Very briefly, add points you did not cover but should have**. But don't forget, the letter must be short and easy to read.

- **Reiterate or elaborate** how you can contribute and solve problems for the company.

- **Express your interest in continuing the dialogue**. A good second-to-last sentence is: "Please consider me an enthusiastic candidate for the position."

- **End with your contact information.** The last sentence should simply begin "If you need more information, please contact me at" then include your phone number and email address.

If, during the interview, you learn that the position does not suit your wants and needs, this is your opportunity to bow out gracefully and professionally. As you do so, try to convert the interviewer into a networking contact so that later you can explore other avenues inside and outside the company. In this case, your letter should always be followed by a phone call. Your letter is your official notice that you are not going to pursue the position any farther. Your phone call establishes that you really do want to have an ongoing relationship with the contact and your words weren't just a formality.

 Optimism is the acquired habit of expecting good things to happen. An optimistic person is not a mere "wishful thinker." Optimism includes being aware of the opportunity that a challenge presents, the knowledge of his or her own ability to affect the outcome, and confidence in his or her ability to enlist the help of others.

For example, when an optimistic woman loses a job, after dealing with the blow emotionally—which admittedly can be very hard—she gets up and gets to work with determination and confidence. Why? She knows she can grow professionally by going through the job search preparation process. She sees that she could end up with an even better job. She knows she has found jobs before and has the ability to find another. And she knows her friends, family and professional network contacts will support her as she goes about seeking a new job.

The PRE-INTERVIEW PLANNING Form

INITIAL CONTACT

Date of Initial Contact: _____

Initial Contact Type (LinkedIn, networking event): _____

Company: _____

City/State: _____

Phone: _____

Email: _____

Position: _____

Company's Main Product/ Service: _____

Company Contact Name/Title: _____

Additional Contact(s): _____

INTERVIEW DETAILS

Interview Address: _____

Date: _____

Interviewer Name: _____

Interviewer Contact Info: _____

Additional Interviewer(s): _____

If at a hotel/restaurant, reservation is under what name: _____

What is the interviewer's role? (direct report, recruiter): _____

If hired, who would you report to? _____

INTERVIEW STRATEGY

How are you relevant for the position? _____

_____

_____

_____

Describe relevant accomplishments: _____

_____

_____

_____

_____

Additional points: _____

_____

_____

_____

The POST-INTERVIEW REVIEW Form

Immediately after the interview, write down everything you can remember about the following details.

INTERVIEW DETAILS

Company: _____

Interview Address: _____

Date: _____

Interviewer Name: _____

Interviewer Contact Info: _____

Additional Interviewer(s): _____

If at a hotel/restaurant, reservation is under what name? _____

What is the interviewer's role? (direct report, recruiter): _____

If hired, who would you report to?: _____

INTERVIEW NOTES

The Position—Special Duties/Responsibilities:_____

_____

_____

The Position—Priorities:_____

_____

_____

_____

The Person—What is the Interviewer looking for? _____

_____

_____

_____

The Company—Goals/Outlook/Philosophy:_____

_____

_____

_____

Cast of Characters—Who Were They? Your Reactions To Them?

_____

_____

_____

Chapter 7: Interview Techniques

The Material (Answers)—What did you tell them? _____

_____

_____

_____

What did you leave out? _____

_____

_____

Information/Clues You Picked Up:_____

_____

_____

Did the interviewer dwell on any one subject or ask a question more than once?

_____

_____

_____

Next Steps:_____

_____

_____

_____

Additional information you'd like to give the interviewer (via email, phone, or follow-up interview):_____

_____

_____

PERFORMANCE NOTES

Your Strengths:_____

_____

_____

_____

Your Weaknesses: :_____

_____

_____

_____

Sample Follow-Up Letter

In this example, the writer has picked up the importance of "Family Atmosphere" which Mr. Cisco mentioned several times during the interview.

Dear Mr. Cisco,

I enjoyed meeting with you yesterday and having the opportunity to learn more about The Cisco Company and your future business plans. I believe we are in agreement that my technical abilities meet with your requirement for the position of Director of Information Services.

What is of equal importance to me is your desire to maintain a family atmosphere within the company. This style of interpersonal relationships is precisely what I have been seeking.

Please consider me an enthusiastic candidate for the position. If you need additional information or clarification, please contact me at (999) 444-5555 or JECitizen@gmail.com.

Sincerely,

Judith E. Citizen.

CHAPTER 8: INTERVIEW QUESTIONS

"A job interview is not a test of your knowledge but your ability to use it at the right time." — *Anonymous*

In This Chapter:

✓ *Remember to listen to the interview questions, take time to think, give concise answers, and be positive*

✓ *If you don't know the real needs of the position and the company, you cannot show how you can fill them. So find them out, even if it means asking the interviewer to explain them*

✓ *Continuously ask yourself, what is the real intent of this question? The real intent ought to relate to whether you are qualified to do the job, fit in at the company and serve its needs*

✓ *Never let yourself get sucked into saying anything negative about your current or past employers, the company with which you are interviewing, or anyone else for that matter, including yourself*

✓ *Avoid discussing salary specifics before you receive an employment offer*

This chapter includes most questions an interviewer is likely to throw at you. Naturally, you will have to tailor your responses to your own background, experience, and achievements. Give yourself many days to work through these questions in writing and then review what you have written over and over again. There is probably no way you could ever remember everything you want to say—nor should you need to—but if you devote yourself to this task, you'll begin to see patterns and become flexible enough to answer confidently no matter what the question. Moreover, you'll be able to shift your response from the questions the interviewer **seems** to be asking to the one he or she *ought* to be asking.

Question-Answering Cheat Sheet

- Be upbeat and positive
- Never talk for more than two minutes
- Rehearse answers frequently so that they will come naturally. Don't try to memorize, just jot down key concepts for each answer
- Find out what the employer seeks, then show you can help them achieve it
- Match your abilities with the needs of them employer
- Sell what the buyer is buying

Question #1: "Tell me about yourself."

Traps: Beware—about 80% of all interviews begin with this 'innocent' question. Many candidates are completely thrown off guard and skewer themselves by rambling, recapping their life story, delving into ancient work history, or relating personal matters. Remember our advice—listen to the question and think about it. Here, your job is to ignore what this question *seems* to be asking and focus on what it is **really** saying: **"Tell me about how you can fit my needs."**

Best Answer: Start with the present, and tell why you are qualified for this position. Remember that the key to all successful interviewing is to match your qualifications to what the interviewer is looking for. **This is the single-most important strategy in executive job hunting.**

So, before you answer this or any question, it's imperative that you:

1. do your homework before the interview to learn as much about the position as possible,

2. then, as early as you can in the interview, ask for a complete description of what the position entails. You might say, "I have a number of accomplishments I'd like to tell you about, but I want to make the best use of our time together and talk directly about your needs. To help me do that, could you tell me more about the most

important priorities of this position? All I know is what I [heard from the recruiter . . . read in the classified ad, etc.]."

You can follow up with a second and possibly third question should you need further clarification. You might ask simply, "And in addition to that?" or, "Is there anything else you see as essential to success in this position?" Surprisingly, it's usually this second or third question that unearths what the interviewer is really after.

This process may not feel comfortable at first, because it is easier to do what you are asked and just answer questions. However, if you practice asking these key questions before giving your answers, the process will begin to feel more natural.

After uncovering what the employer is looking for, explain how the various tasks you've succeeded at before relate directly to the employer's needs. If you succeed, you'll be a perfect match for job.

Question #2: *"What are your greatest strengths?"*

Traps: This question seems like a softball lob, but be prepared. You don't want to come across as egotistical or arrogant. Neither is this a time to be humble.

Best Answer: Prior to any interview, you should have a mentally prepared list, and a specific example or two, chosen from your most recent and most impressive achievements, which illustrate each strength.

Using what you learned from the prior questions, choose those strengths that best match up to what the interviewer seems to require. As a general guideline, the 10 most desirable traits that all employers love to see in executives are:

1. **An achiever** with a proven track record of achievements which match up with the employer's greatest wants and needs.
2. **Intelligence** and "savvy."
3. **A decent human being** who has integrity.
4. **A good fit with the corporate culture** with whom others can feel comfortable.
5. **Positive attitude** and a sense of humor.
6. **A communicator** who can read people, listen, ask questions, and speak well.

7. **Dedication** and willingness to walk the extra mile to achieve excellence.
8. **Focus** with clear goals.
9. **Enthusiasm** about what you do.
10. **A leader** with confidence, a healthy sense of self, and the ability to motivate others to follow you.

Question #3: _"What are your greatest weaknesses?"_

Traps: Beware—this is an "eliminator" question, designed to shorten the candidate list. Any admission of a weakness or fault will earn you an "A" for honesty but an "F" for the interview.

Don't answer the literal questions but address what ought to be the intent behind it. What the interview really wants to know is, do you have any weakness which will make you unable to do an outstanding job?

Passable Answer: Disguise a strength as a weakness. Example: "I sometimes push my people too hard. I like to work with a sense of urgency and may expect others to do so as well."

Drawback: This strategy is better than admitting a flaw, but it's so widely used, it is transparent to any experienced interviewer.

Best Answer: Assure your interviewer that you can think of nothing that would stand in the way of your performing in this position with excellence. Then, quickly review your strongest qualifications. This is another reason why it's so important to get a thorough description of your interviewer's needs before you answer questions.

Example: "Nobody's perfect, but based on what you've told me about this position, I believe that I'd make an outstanding match. I know that when I hire people, I look for two things most of all: Do they have the qualifications and the motivation to do the job well? Everything in my background shows that I have both the qualifications and a strong desire to achieve excellence in whatever I take on. So I can say in all honesty that I see nothing that would cause you even a small concern about my ability or my strong desire to perform this job with excellence."

An **alternate strategy**—if you don't yet know enough about the position to talk about a perfect fit—is instead of confessing a weakness, describe what you like most and like least, making sure that what you like matches up with the most important qualification for success in the position, and what you like least is not essential.

Question #4: "What are your salary expectations?"

Traps: This question may also be phrased as, "What salary are you worth?" or "How much are you making now?" How you answer is critical for future negotiations. Handle it incorrectly and you could blow the job offer or go to work for far less than you might have gotten. Although you do need to know that the position offers a salary that will be acceptable to you, the best time for you to have the conversation about salary is after the offer has been made. The reason is that at that point, they want you.

Best Answer: For maximum salary negotiating power, remember these five guidelines.

1. **Postpone the question.** If your interviewer raises the salary question too early, before you've had a chance to create desire for your qualifications, put him off, saying something like, "Money is important to me, but it is not my main concern. Opportunity and growth are far more important. What I'd rather do, if you don't mind, is explore if I'm right for the position, and then talk about the money. Would that be okay?"

2. **The number one principle of any negotiation is that the side with more information usually wins.** After you've done a thorough job of selling the interviewer, and it's time to talk salary, the secret is to get the employer talking about what he's willing to pay you before you reveal what you are willing to accept. So, when asked about salary, respond by asking, "I'm sure the company has already established a salary range for this position. Could you tell me what that is?" or, "I want an income commensurate with my ability and qualifications. I trust you'll be fair with me. What does the position pay?"

3. **Never bring up salary.** Let the interviewer do it first. Good salespeople sell their products thoroughly before talking price. So should you. Make the interviewer want you first, and your bargaining position will be much stronger. The reason why this works is because of the dynamics of hiring. At first, you are courting them. Once they want you, they are doing the courting.

4. **Know beforehand what you're willing to accept.** To know what's reasonable, research the job market and this position for any relevant salary information. Remember that most executives look for a 20% to

25% pay boost when they switch jobs. If you're grossly underpaid now, you may want even more than that.

5. **Maximize your current salary.** Never lie about what you make, but feel free to include the estimated cost of all your fringe benefits and payroll deductions, which is 25% to 50% more than your present "cash-only" salary. So, if you make $80K, you can honestly say, "my current package is worth approximately $120,000." Then you might say, "I would be comfortable with $100K gross salary." This might cost them $150K total, but you don't need to point that out.

Question #5: *"Why are you leaving (or did you leave) your previous position?"*

Traps: Never badmouth your previous industry, company, board, boss, staff, employees, or customers. This rule is inviolable—Never be negative! Again, any mud you sling will ultimately land on you.

Furthermore, avoid phrases like "personality clash," "didn't get along," or words that cast a shadow on your competence, integrity, or temperament.

Best Answer: This is something you would have considered earlier in your job search process when you began networking (see Chapter Five). Here, we will just summarize.

If you currently have a job, say so and explain what you are hoping to find in a new position.

If you do <u>not</u> currently have a job, it may be appropriate to try to deflect the reason from you personally by explaining that you left because of a takeover, merger, downsizing, and so on. If this is not the case, be prepared with a brief answer that describes your desire to find a position with added responsibility, more opportunities, a larger salary, or other missing quality you are seeking in your specific situation.

Question #6: *What about this position appeals to you?*

Traps: The interviewer is listening for an answer that indicates you have given some thought into your search and are not sending our resumes just because there is a job opening.

Best Response: Identify a couple of key factors that you consider would make this a great job for you. This would be a great time for you to demonstrate your commitment to your values and how they apply to your job search. For example:

- "In looking at companies I'd like to work for, I found that yours has the type of environment that I would excel in. Additionally, your company's mission statement speaks to me, and I know I would be excited about being part of what this company does."

- "I love customer support because I love the constant human interaction and the satisfaction that comes from helping someone solve a problem."

Question #7: *"Why should I hire you?"*

Traps: Believe it or not, many candidates are unprepared for this question.

Best Answer: Whether your interviewer asks you this question explicitly or not, this may be most important question of your interview because he must answer it favorably in his own mind before he will offer the job to you. Walk through the position's requirements and describe how you fulfill each one.

Example: "As I understand your needs, you are first and foremost looking for someone who can manage the sales and marketing of your trade book publishing division. Is that right? This is where I've spent almost all of my career: 18 years of experience in trade books. I believe that I know the right contacts, methods, principles, and successful management techniques to be successful in this position."

"You also need someone who can expand your book distribution channels. Right? In my prior post, my innovative promotional ideas doubled, and then tripled, the number of outlets selling our books. I'm confident I can do the same for you."

Question #8: *"Aren't you overqualified for this position?"*

Traps: What may really be behind this question is a fear that you'll grow dissatisfied and leave as soon as something better comes along. Anything you can say to demonstrate the sincerity of your commitment to the employer and to reassure him that you're looking to stay for the long term will help you overcome this objection.

Best Answer: Assuming you are highly qualified, don't view this question as a sign of imminent rejection. It's an invitation to teach the interviewer a new way to think about the situation, seeing advantages instead of drawbacks. For example:

- "I recognize the job market for what it is—a marketplace. Like any marketplace, it's subject to the laws of supply and demand. So 'overqualified' can be a relative term, depending on how tight the job market is. And right now, it's very tight. I understand and accept that."

- "I also believe that there could be very positive benefits for both of us in this match."

- "Because of my unusually strong experience in management, I could start to contribute right away, perhaps much faster than someone who'd have to be brought along more slowly."

- "There's also the tens of thousands of dollars' worth of training that other companies have invested to give me. You'd be getting all that value without having to pay an extra dime for it. With someone who has yet to acquire that experience, he'd have to gain it on your nickel."

- "I could also help you in many things they don't teach in business school, for example, how to hire, train, and motivate employees. When it comes to knowing how to work well with people and how to get the most out of them, there's just no substitute for what you learn over many years of front-line experience. Your company would gain all this, too."

- "From my side, there are strong benefits as well. Right now, I'm unemployed. I want to work, very much, and the position you have here is exactly what I love to do and am best at. I'd be happy doing this work, and that's what matters most to me. A lot more than money or title."

- "Most important, I'm looking to make a long-term commitment in my career now. I've had enough of job-hunting and want a permanent spot. I also know that if I perform this job with excellence, other opportunities cannot help but open up for me right here. In time, I'll find many other ways to help this company, and, in doing so, help myself. I really am looking to make a long- term commitment."

Question #9: "Where do you see yourself in three years? In six? In ten?"

Traps: One reason interviewers ask this question is to see if you're just settling for this position, using it merely as a stopover until something better comes along. Another reason is trying to gauge your level of ambition.

If you're too specific, i.e., naming the promotions you someday hope to win, you'll sound presumptuous. If you're too vague, you'll seem rudderless.

Best Answer: Reassure your interviewer that you're looking to make a long-term commitment, to exactly this type of position. As for your future, you are confident that you can perform the job at hand with excellence and future opportunities will present themselves.

Question #10: "Describe your ideal company, location and job."

Traps: This is often asked by an experienced interviewer who thinks you may be overqualified, but knows better than to show his hand by posing his objection directly. So, he'll use this question instead, to find out if the candidate is for something other than the position at hand.

Best Answer: The only right answer is to describe what this company is offering, being sure to make your answer believable with specific reasons, stated with sincerity, why each quality represented by this opportunity is attractive to you.

Remember, if you're coming from a company that's the leader in its field or from a glamorous or much-admired company, industry, city or position, your interviewer and his company may well have an "Avis" complex. That is, they may feel a bit defensive about being "second best".

This anxiety could be there even though you've done nothing to inspire it. You must go out of your way to assuage such worry, even if it's not expressed, by putting the company's virtues high in the list of what you're looking for, providing credible reasons for wanting these qualities.

Career & Experience Questions

Question # 11: *"Why do you want to work at our company?"*

Traps: This question tests whether you've done your homework about the firm.

Best Answer: Again, discuss specific qualities of the company that make it a place where you would like to work.

Best sources for researching your target company: annual reports, the corporate newsletter, contacts you know at the company, its suppliers, advertisements, articles about the company in the trade press, and the company's own website.

Question #12: *"What are your career options right now?"*

Traps: The interviewer is trying to figure out your motives.

Best Answer: Prepare for this question by thinking of how you can position yourself as a desired commodity. If you are still working, describe the possibilities at your present firm and why, though you're greatly appreciated there, you're looking for something more, whether it is challenge, money, or responsibility. Also mention that you're seriously exploring opportunities with one or two other firms.

If you're no longer working, you can talk about other employment possibilities you're actively exploring. But do this with a light touch, speaking only in general terms, avoiding sounding either manipulative or coy.

Question #13: *"Why have you had so many jobs?"*

Traps: Your interviewer fears you may leave this position quickly, as you have others. He's concerned you may be unreliable or a "problem person" who can't get along with others.

Best Answer: First, before you even get to the interview stage, you should try to minimize your image as a job hopper. If there are several entries on your resume of less than one year, consider eliminating the less important ones and specify the time spent at previous positions in rounded years, not in months and years.

Example: Instead of presenting three positions as in the first column below, you would show them as in the second column:

6/2002—3/2003, Position A	2002—2003, Position A
4/2003—12/2003, Position B	2004—2007, Position C
1/2004—9/2007, Position C	

In other words, you would drop Position B altogether. Notice what a difference this makes in reducing your image as a job hopper. In the interview, describe each position as part of an overall pattern of growth.
Be careful not to blame other people for your frequent changes. Rather, attribute certain changes to conditions beyond your control (i.e., because of an impending merger).

If possible, show that your job changes were more frequent earlier in your career, while you were establishing yourself, rounding out your skills, and looking for the right career path. At this stage, you're more interested in the best long-term opportunities.

You might also focus on the jobs at which you stayed the longest and describe that this type of situation is what you're looking for now.

<u>Question #14</u>: *"How could you have improved your career progress?"*

Traps: This is a variation on the question, "If you could, how would you live your life over?"

Best Answer: You're generally quite happy with your career progress. Maybe, if you had known something earlier in life— impossible to have foreseen at the time, such as the booming growth in a branch of your industry, or a corporate downsizing that would phase out your last job— you might have moved in a certain direction sooner. But all things considered, you take responsibility for where you are, how you've gotten there, where you're going. You harbor no regrets.

<u>Question #15</u>: *"You've been with your firm for a long time. Won't it be hard switching to a new company?"*

Traps: Your interviewer is worried you are an old dog who won't be able to learn new tricks.

Best Answer: To overcome this objection, you must point to the many ways you have grown and adapted to changing conditions in your present firm. It has not been a static situation. Highlight the different responsibilities you've held, the wide array of new situations you've faced and conquered. As a result, you've learned to adapt to changes quickly, to whatever is thrown at you, and you thrive on the stimulation of new challenges.

To further assure the interviewer, describe similarities between the new position and your prior one. Explain that you would be quite comfortable working there, since their needs and your skills make the perfect match.

Question #16: "May I contact your present employer for a reference?"

Traps: If you're trying to keep your job search private, this is the last thing you want, but you don't want to look like you're hiding something.

Best Answer: Express that you'd like to keep your search private for now, but that at the appropriate time, it will be perfectly okay to contact your references.

Question #17: "What's the most difficult part about being a [job title]?"

Traps: Unless you phrase your answer properly, your interviewer may conclude that whatever you identify as "difficult" is where you're weak.

Best Answer: First, redefine "difficult" to be "challenging," which is more positive. Then, identify an area everyone in your profession considers challenging and in which you excel. Describe the process you follow that enables you to get splendid results, and be specific about those results.

Example: "I think every sales manager finds it challenging to motivate the troops in a recession. But that's probably the strongest test of a top sales manager. I feel this is one area where I excel. When I see the first sign that sales may slip or that sales force motivation is flagging because of a downturn in the economy, here's the plan I put into action immediately." Follow this by a description of each step in the process, and most importantly, in the exceptional results you've achieved.

Question #18: "Have you considered starting your own business?"

Traps: If you say "yes" and then enthuse over your dream firm, you could be perceived as a loose cannon in a larger company, too entrepreneurial to make a good team player. Or you might be perceived as someone who had to settle for corporate life because you couldn't make a go of your own business.

Also, too much enthusiasm in answering "yes" could rouse the paranoia of a small company, indicating that you may plan to go out on your own soon, perhaps taking some key accounts or trade secrets with you.

On the other hand, if you answer, "no, never" you could be perceived as a security-minded drone who never dreamed a big dream.

Best Answer: Again, it's best to gauge this company's corporate culture before answering, and be honest—which doesn't mean you have to share your fantasy of the franchise or bed-and-breakfast you someday plan to open. In addition, if what you really want right now is your own business, why aren't you pursuing that instead of looking for a job?

In general, if the corporate culture is that of a large, formal, military-style structure, minimize any indication that you'd love to have your own business. You might say, "Oh, I have given it a thought once or twice, but my whole career has been in larger organizations. That's where I've excelled and where I want to be."

If the corporate culture is closer to the free-wheeling, everybody's a deal-maker variety, then emphasize that in a firm like this, you can virtually get the best of both worlds: the excitement of seeing your own ideas and plans take shape, combined with the resources and stability of a well-established organization. Sounds like the perfect environment to you.

Question #19: "What was the toughest part of your last job?"

Traps: This is slightly different from Question #17 because this asks what you personally have found most difficult in your last position. This question is harder to redefine into something positive. Your interviewer will assume that whatever you found toughest before may give you a problem in your new position.

Best Answer: State that there was nothing in your prior position that you found overly difficult and let your answer go at that. If pressed to expand your answer, you could describe the aspects of the position you enjoyed more than others, making sure that you express maximum enjoyment for those tasks most important to the open position, and you enjoyed least those tasks that are unimportant to the position at hand.

Question #20: *"How would you define success and how do you measure up to your own definitions?"*

Traps: This seems like an obvious enough question, yet many executives, unprepared for it, fumble the ball.

Best Answer: Give a well-accepted definition of success that leads right into your own stellar collection of achievements, which tie into what the company you are interviewing with is looking for.

Example: "The best definition that I've come across is that success is the progressive realization of a worthy goal. As to how I would measure up to that definition, I would consider myself both successful and fortunate."

Then summarize your career goals and how your achievements have indeed represented a progressive path toward realizing them. Then, you can relate what you still want to do with what this company needs done.

Question #21: *"Looking back on your last position, have you done your best work?"*

Traps: Tricky question. Answer "Absolutely!" and it can seem like your best work is behind you. Answer, "No, my best work is ahead of me," and it can seem as if you didn't give it your all.

Best Answer: To cover both possible paths this question can take, your answer should state that you always put forth your best efforts. Then, highlight your strongest qualifications.

Decision-Making & Stress Questions

Question #22: *"Why haven't you found a new position by now?"*

Traps: A tough question if you've been on the bench a long time.

Best Answer: Remain steady and professional as you emphasize factors that have prolonged your job search, preferably due to your own choice.

Examples:

- "After my job was terminated, I made a conscious decision not to jump on the first opportunities to come along. In my life, I've found that I can always turn a negative into a positive if I try hard enough. This is what I was determined to do. I decided to take whatever time I needed to think through what I do best, what I want most to do, where I'd like to do it, and then identity those companies that could offer such an opportunity."

- "Also, in all honesty, you have to factor in the recession (consolidation, stabilization) in the (banking, financial services, manufacturing, advertising) industry."

- "So, between my being selective and the companies in our industry downsizing, the process has taken time. But, in the end, I'm convinced that when I do find the right match, all that careful evaluation from both sides of the desk will have been well worthwhile for both the company that hires me and myself as well. And here's why I think your company and I are a good match . . ."

Question #23: *"Can you work under pressure?"*

Traps: An easy question, but you want to make your answer believable.

Best Answer: "Absolutely." Then prove it with a vivid example of a goal achieved or project accomplished under pressure.

Question #24: *"What makes you angry?"*

Traps: Remember to stop for a moment to consider your answer to this question.

Best Answer: Give an answer that's suited to both your personality and the management style of the firm. In this instance, the homework you've done about the company and its style can particularly help in your choice of words.

Examples:

If you are a reserved person or the corporate culture is coolly professional:

"I'm an even-tempered and positive person by nature, and I believe this helps me a great deal in keeping my department running smoothly, harmoniously and with a genuine esprit de corps. I believe in communicating clearly what's expected, getting people's commitment to those goals and then following up continuously to check progress. If anyone or anything is going off-track, I want to know about it early. If, after that kind of open communication and follow-up, someone isn't getting the job done, I'll want to know why. If there's no good reason, then I'll get impatient and angry, and take appropriate steps from there. But if you hire good people, motivate them to strive for excellence and then follow up constantly, it almost never gets to that stage."

If you are feisty by nature or the position calls for a tough straw boss:

"You know what makes me angry? People who . . . " Then fill in the blank with the most objectionable traits for this type of position: for example, people who don't pull their own weight, who are negative, who lie and so on.

Question #25: *"What would you do if a fellow executive on your own corporate level was not pulling his weight, and this was hurting your department?"*

Traps: This question and other hypothetical ones test your sense of human relations and how you might handle office politics.

Best Answer: Try to gauge the political style of the firm and be guided accordingly. In general, fall back on universal principles of effective human relations—which, in the end, embody the way you would like to be treated in a similar circumstance.

Example: "Good human relations would call for me to go directly to the person and explain the situation, to try to enlist his help in a constructive, positive solution. If I sensed resistance, I would be as persuasive as I know how to in order to explain the benefits we all gain from working together and the problems we, the company, and our customers experience if we don't."

Possible Follow-Up Question: *"And what would you do if he still didn't change his ways?"*

Answers:

- "One thing I wouldn't do is let the problem slide, because it would only get worse, and overlooking it would set a bad precedent. I would try again and again and again, in whatever way I could to solve the problem, involving wider and wider circles of people, both above and below the offending executive and including my own boss, if necessary, so that everyone involved can see the rewards for teamwork and the drawbacks of non-cooperation."

- "I've never yet come across a situation that couldn't be resolved by harnessing others in a determined, constructive effort."

Question #26: "Give me an example of your creativity."

Traps: This is another question that requires advance preparation.

Best Answer: Remember from Question #2 that you should commit to memory a list of your greatest and most recent achievements, ever ready on the tip of your tongue.

If you have such a list, it's easy to present any of your achievements in light of the quality the interviewer is asking about. For example, the smashing success you orchestrated at last year's trade show could be used as an example of creativity, or analytical ability, or your ability to manage.

Question #27: "What makes you feel anxious?"

Traps: Admitting to high levels of anxiety may raise red flags. However, saying that you never worry doesn't sound credible.

Best Answer: Redefine "anxiety" in a way that it doesn't reflect negatively on you.

Example: "I wouldn't call it anxiety or worry, but I am a strongly goal-oriented person, and I keep turning over in my mind anything that seems to be keeping me from achieving those goals, until I find a solution. That's part of my tenacity, I suppose."

Question #28: "What is the toughest challenge you've ever faced?"

Traps: Don't cite an example from the too distant past.

Best Answer: This is an easy question if you're prepared. Have a recent example that demonstrates either:

- A quality most important to the job at hand; or
- A quality that is always in demand, such as leadership, initiative, managerial skill, persuasiveness, courage, persistence, intelligence, etc.

The interviewer wants to know whether you have ever been in a tough situation similar to tough situations you might face in this new position. Consequently, it's perfectly honest to talk about how you exercised some virtue in another situation which could be called for in a hypothetical, future situation at this firm.

Question #29: _"Looking back, what would you do differently in your life?"_

Traps: This question is usually asked to uncover any life-influencing mistakes, regrets, disappointments, or problems that may continue to affect your personality and performance.

It is good for you to realize—without saying anything to the interviewer—that this question is an irrelevant one. The purpose of the interview is to ascertain how qualified you are for this position, not to philosophize about your life.

You do not want to give the interviewer anything negative to remember you by, such as some great personal or career disappointment, even long ago, that you wish you could have avoided.

Best Answer: Indicate that you are a content, optimistic person who makes a decision then moves on.

Example: "I believe I made the best choices I could at the time; I wouldn't change a thing."

Question #30: _"Could you have done better in your last job?"_

Traps: This is no time for true confessions of major—or even minor—problems. Again, never be negative or put yourself down.

Best Answer: Say that you have always done your best.

Example: "I suppose with the benefit of hindsight you can always find things to do better, of course, but off the top of my head, I can't think of anything of major consequence."

If more explanation seems necessary, describe a situation that wasn't ideal not because of you but external conditions beyond your control.

For example, describe the disappointment you felt with a test campaign, new product launch, a merger, etc., which looked promising at first but led to underwhelming results. "I wish we could have known at the start what we later found out [about the economy turning, the marketplace changing, etc.], but since we couldn't, we just had to go for it. And from it we learned..."

Question #31: *"Tell me about the most boring job you've ever had."*

Traps: You give a very memorable description of a very boring job. Results? You become associated with this boring job in the interviewer's mind.

Best Answers: (1) You had some dull jobs early in your life, say in high school or during summers in college, but that was because they didn't call on you to think, exercise judgment, or be creative. That is one reason you went to college and entered this meaningful field. Or better, (2) You've never allowed yourself to grow bored with a job, and have pursued positions that are challenging.

Example: "Perhaps I've been fortunate, but I've never found myself bored with any job I've ever held. I've always enjoyed hard work. As with actors who feel there are no small parts, I also believe that in every company or department there are exciting challenges and intriguing problems crying out for energetic and enthusiastic solutions. If you're bored, it's probably because you're not challenging yourself to tackle those problems right under your nose."

Question #32: *"Why aren't you earning more money at this stage of your career?"*

Traps: This question assumes you have revealed your salary history this early in the process, something you want to avoid. You don't want to give the impression that money is not important to you, yet you want to explain if your salary may be a little below industry standards.

Best Answer: You like to make money, but other factors are even more important.

Example: "Making money is important to me, and but I have taken positions with lower salaries [to increase experience/knowledge in a certain area/for personal reasons, etc.]."

Then be prepared to be specific about what your ideal position and company would be like, matching them as closely as possible to the opportunity at hand.

Goals & Vision Question

Question #33: _"What are your goals?"_

Traps: Not having any … or having only vague generalities, not highly specific goals. If you're vague about your career and personal goals, it could be a big turnoff to many people you may encounter in your job search.

Best Answer: Many executives in a position to hire you are strong believers in goal-setting: it's one of the reasons they've achieved so much. They like to hire their kind—other goal-setters.

But begin by asking, "Are you interested in my career goals or my life goals in general?" Be ready to discuss your goals for each major area of your life: career, personal development and learning, physical (how you stay healthy) and community service. If your interviewer is clearly a religious person, you could very briefly and generally allude to your spiritual goals, showing you are a well- balanced individual with your values in the right order.

Be prepared to describe each goal, why it is important to you, time periods you're allotting for accomplishment and milestones that show your progress. But do this concisely, as you never want to talk for more than two minutes straight before letting your interviewer back into the conversation.

Supervising & Staffing Questions

Question #34: _"Do you have the stomach to fire people? Have you had experience in firing many people?"_

Traps: This "innocent" question could be a trap door which sends you down a chute and lands you in a heap of dust outside the front door. Why? Because its real intent is not just to see if you've got the stomach to fire, but also to uncover if you've fired a lot of people. If you have, this could indicate you have poor judgment in hiring.

So, don't rise to the bait by boasting about how many you've fired, unless you're prepared to explain why it was beyond your control and not the result of your poor hiring procedures or foul temperament.

Best Answer: Describe the rational and sensible management process you follow in both hiring and firing.

Example: "My whole management approach is to hire the best people I can find, train them well, get them excited and proud to be part of our team, and then work with them to achieve our goals together. If you do all of that right, especially hiring the right people, I've found you don't have to fire very often. So, with me, firing is the last resort. But when it's got to be done, it's got to be done, and the faster and cleaner the better. A poor employee can wreak terrible havoc in undermining the morale of an entire team of good people. When there's no other way, I've found it's better for all concerned to act fairly but decisively in getting rid of offenders who won't change their ways."

Question #35: "What would you say to your boss if he's crazy about an idea, but you think it stinks?"

Traps: If you are thrown a curveball question, think for a moment about why it is hard to answer. This is actually a question that pits two values against each another: loyalty and honesty. Notice how the question is a real dilemma until you uncover the underlying intent. It is not a bad idea to ask the interviewer: "It sounds like you are asking me how I would balance loyalty and honesty. Is that correct?"

Best Answer: In any conflict among values, always choose integrity.

Example: "I believe that when evaluating anything, it's important to emphasize the positive. What do I like about this idea? Then, if I have reservations, I certainly want to point them out, as specifically, objectively and factually as I can. After all, the most important thing I owe my boss is honesty. If he can't count on me for that, then everything else I may do or say would be questionable in his eyes. But I also want to express my thoughts in a constructive way. So, my goal in this could be to see if my boss and I could make his idea even stronger and more appealing, so that it effectively overcomes any initial reservation I or others may have about it... Of course, if he overrules me and says, 'No, let's do it my way,' then I owe him my full and enthusiastic support to make it work as best as it can."

Question #36: "What do you look for when you hire people?"

Trap: Being unprepared for this question.

Best Answer: Speak your own thoughts here, but for the best answer, weave them around the important qualifications for any position:

- Can the person do the work: In other words, is he qualified?

- Will the person do the work: That is, is he motivated?

- Will the person fit in with the corporate culture as an effective part of our team?

"Job Fit" Related Questions

Question #37: "What changes would you make if you came on board?"

Traps: Watch out! This question can derail your candidacy faster than a bomb under the tracks and just as you're about to be hired!

(1) Answer this question carefully. (2) No matter how comfortable you may feel with your interviewer, you are still an outsider. No one, including your interviewer, likes to think that a know-it-all outsider is going to come in, and turn the place upside down. (3) It takes time to know the operation's strengths, weaknesses, key people, financial condition, methods of operation, etc.

Best Answer: You will study everything the company is doing before making any recommendations or taking any actions.

Example: "Well, I wouldn't be a very good doctor if I gave my diagnosis before the examination. Should you hire me, as I hope you will, I'd want to take a good, hard look at everything you're doing and understand why it's being done that way. I'd like to have in-depth meetings with you and the other key people to get a deeper grasp of what you feel you're doing right and what could be improved. From what you've told me so far, the areas of greatest concern to you are..." Name them and ask if these are, in fact, his major concerns. If so, then reaffirm how your experience in meeting similar needs elsewhere might prove very helpful.

Question #38: "I'm concerned that you don't have as much experience as we'd like in..."

Traps: The interviewer mostly likes what he sees but has doubts about one key area. If you can assure him on this point, the job may be yours.

Best Answer: This question is related to "The Fatal Flaw" (Question #51), but here the concern is not that you are totally missing some qualification, such as CPA certification, but rather that your experience is light in some area.

Before going into any interview, try to identify the weakest aspects of your candidacy from this company's point of view. Then prepare the best answer you possibly can to shore up your defenses.

Use your master strategy of uncovering the employer's greatest wants and needs and then matching them with your strengths. More specifically, when the interviewer poses an objection like this one, you should agree on the importance of this qualification; then show how and why your strength in this area may actually be greater than the resume indicates; and finally point out that when this strength is added to your others, your overall combination of qualifications will serve the company well. This shifts focus away from a specific area and puts it on the unique combination of strengths you offer.

Question #39: "What do you see as the proper role of a good [job title you're seeking]?"

Traps: These and other "proper role" questions are designed to test your understanding of your place in the big picture of your department, company, community and profession, as well as the proper role each of these entities should play in the bigger picture.

The most thoughtful individuals and companies frequently ask this question. It might also be asked by someone concerned that you're coming from a place with a radically different corporate culture, such as moving from a big government bureaucracy to an aggressive, smaller company.

The most frequent mistake candidates make in answering questions is simply not being prepared and, thus, appearing as if they've never given any kind of thought to these questions. Another mistake is in phrasing an answer best suited to their current organization's culture instead of the hiring company's culture.

Best Answer: Identify three to six qualities which you feel are most important to success in your new role. Then commit your responses to memory. If you can, relate those qualities in terms of what the culture of the firm appears to be.

Question #40: The Hypothetical Problem

Traps: Sometimes an interviewer will describe a difficult situation and ask, "How would you handle this?" Since it's virtually impossible to have all the facts in front of you from such a short presentation, don't fall into the trap of trying to solve this problem and giving your verdict on the spot. It will make your decision-making process seem woefully inadequate.

Best Answer: Instead of giving a specific answer to a hypothetical problem, describe the rational, methodical process you would follow in analyzing this problem, consulting with key people, generating possible solutions, choosing the best course of action and monitoring the results.

Remember, for all such "what would you do?" questions, always describe your process or working methods, and you'll never go too far wrong.

Question #41: "How are you at selling? Okay, sell me this stapler."

Traps: Some interviewers—especially business owners and hard-charging executives in marketing-driven companies—feel that good salesmanship is essential for any key position and ask for an instant demonstration of your skill. Be ready. Below is a short "master class" on salesmanship.

Best Answer: Let's say your interviewer picks up the stapler and demands, "Sell this to me." You are going to demonstrate the proven master principle of sales: Find out what people want, then show them how to get it.

Example:

"Well, a good salesman must know both his product and his prospect before he sells anything. If I were selling this, I'd first get to know everything I could about it, all of its features and benefits...."

"Then, if my goal were to sell it to you, I would do some research on how you might use a fine stapler like this. The best way to do that is by asking questions. May I ask you a few questions?..."

"Just out of curiosity, if you didn't already have a stapler like this, why would you want one? And in addition to that? Any other reasons? Anything else?..."

"And would you want such a stapler to be reliable? Hold a good supply of staples?" Ask more questions that point to the features this stapler has.

Once you've asked these questions, make your presentation, citing all the features and benefits of this stapler and why it's exactly what the interviewer just told you he's looking for.

Then close with, "Just out of curiosity, what would you consider a reasonable price for a quality stapler like this . . . a stapler you could have right now and would [repeat all the problems the stapler could solve for him]?" Whatever he says, unless it's zero, say, "Okay, we've got a deal."

If your interviewer tests you by fighting every step of the way, denying that he even wants such an item, don't combat him. Take the product away from him by saying, "Mr. Prospect, I'm delighted you've told me right up front that there's no way you'd ever want this stapler. As you well know, the first rule of the most productive salespeople in any field is to meet the needs of people who really need and want our products, and it just wastes everyone's time if we try to force it on those who don't. And I certainly wouldn't want to waste your time. But we sell many items. Is there any product on this desk you would very much like to own . . . just one item?"

When he points something out, repeat the process above.

Work Habits & Former Bosses

Question #42: *"Have you been absent from work for more than a few days in any previous position?"*

Traps: If you've had a problem, you can't lie. You could easily be found out. Yet admitting an attendance problem could raise many red flags.

Best Answer: If you have had no problem, emphasize your excellent and consistent attendance record throughout your career.

Also describe how important you believe such consistent attendance is for a key executive, why it's up to you to set an example of dedication, and why there's just no substitute for being there with your people to keep the operation running smoothly, answer questions and handle problems and crises as they arise.

If you do have a past attendance problem, you want to minimize it, making it clear that it was an exceptional circumstance and that its cause has been corrected.

To smoothly drive this point home, give the same answer as above, but preface it with something like, "Other than being out last year [or whenever] because of [your reason, which is now in the past], I have never had a problem and have enjoyed an excellent attendance record throughout my career. Furthermore, I believe consistent attendance is important because..." Then pick up the rest of the answer as outlined above.

Question #43: *"How do you feel about working nights and weekends?"*

Traps: Feeling like you need to agree to off-hours in order to earn the offer.

Best Answer: First, if you're a confirmed workaholic, you could say that this kind of schedule is just your style. Add that your family understands it and know you get great satisfaction from your work.

If, however, you prefer a more balanced lifestyle, answer this question with another: "What's the norm for your best people here?"

If the hours still sound unrealistic for you, ask, "Do you have any top people who perform exceptionally for you, but who also have families and like to get home in time to see them at night?" Chances are, the company does, and this associates you with this other, "top-performers-who-leave-no-later-than-six" group.

Depending on the answer, be honest about how you would fit into the picture. If all those extra hours make you uncomfortable, say so, but phrase your response positively.

Example: "I love my work and do it exceptionally well. I think the results speak for themselves, especially in [mention your two or three qualifications of greatest interest to the employer]." Remember, this is what he wants most, not a workaholic with weak credentials. "Not only would I bring these qualities to the position, but I've built my whole career on working not just hard, but smart. I think you'll find me one of the most productive people here. I do have a family who likes to see me after work and on weekends. They add balance and richness to my life, which in turn helps me to be happy and productive at work. If I could handle some of that extra work at home in the evenings or on weekends, that would be ideal. You'd be getting a person of exceptional productivity who meets your needs with very strong credentials. And I'd be able to handle some of the heavy workload at home where I can be under the same roof as my family. Everybody would win."

Question #44: *"Are you willing to relocate or travel?"*

Traps: Answer with a flat "no" and you may slam the door shut on this opportunity. But what if you'd really prefer not to relocate or travel, yet wouldn't want to lose the job offer over it?

Best Answer: Your research ought to have uncovered whether relocation or travel went along with this position. If you absolutely cannot relocate or travel extensively, you would not have applied, so this answer assumes either you are just learning about this or you have strong reservations about travelling or relocating. If your answer is an unqualified no, then say so and explain why. If it is not an absolute no, find out where you might have to relocate and how much travel may be involved. Then respond to the question.

There are **two schools of thought** on how to answer.

One advises you to keep your reservations to yourself and offer a simple "yes" to keep your options open. You may get such a great offer that your objections will melt away.

Also, by the time the offer is actually made, you may have other offers and can make a more informed decision. In three months, having a job which requires travelling three days a week might look a lot better than no job which lets you say home.

A second way to handle this question is to voice a reservation, but assert that you'd be open to relocating, or traveling, for the right opportunity. If the company really wants you, giving this answer can induce them to sweeten the pot or hire you in a capacity which doesn't entail relocation or extensive travel.

Question #45: _"How many hours a week do you normally work?"_

Traps: You don't want to give a specific number. Make it too low, and you may not measure up. Too high, and you'll forever feel guilty about sneaking out the door at 5:15 p.m.

Best Answer: If you are, in fact, a workaholic, and you sense this company would like that trait, say that you're a confirmed workaholic, that you often work nights and weekends. Your family accepts this characteristic of your professional life because it makes you fulfilled.

If you aren't a workaholic, then state that you've always worked hard and put in the hours necessary. It goes with the territory.

**Question #46**: "Tell me honestly about the strong and weak points of your previous boss."

Traps: Skillful interviewers sometimes make it almost irresistible to open up and air a little dirty laundry from your previous position. **Don't do it.**

Best Answer: Remember one of the true golden rules: Never be negative. Stress only the good points, no matter how charmingly you're invited to be critical.

Your interviewer doesn't care a whit about your previous boss. He wants to find out how loyal and positive you are, and whether you'll criticize him behind his back if pressed to do so. This question is your opportunity to demonstrate that you are professional and loyal to those with whom you work.

Character & Personal Questions

**Question #47**: "Would you lie for the company?"

Traps: This is another question that pits two values against one another, in this case loyalty vs. integrity.

Best Answer: "I would never do anything to hurt the company."

If aggressively pressed to choose between two competing values, always choose personal integrity.

**Question #48**: "How do you feel about reporting to a younger person [or someone of a different gender or race]."

Traps: It's a shame that some interviewers feel the need to ask this question, but many understand the reality that prejudices still exist among some job candidates, and it's better to try to flush them out beforehand.

The trap here is that in today's politically sensitized environments, even a well-intentioned answer can raise red flags. Avoid anything which smacks of a patronizing or insensitive attitude, such as, "I think 'they' can make terrific bosses."

Best Answer: State that the age [or gender, race, etc.] of the person you report to would certainly make no difference to you. Whoever has that position has obviously earned it and knows their job well. Both the person and the position are fully deserving of respect.

Question #49: *"Give me an example of when your work has been criticized."*

Traps: This is a tough question because it's a more clever and subtle way to get you to admit a weakness. You can't dodge it by pretending you've never been criticized—everybody has been criticized. Yet it can be quite damaging to start admitting potential faults and failures.

This question is also intended to probe how well you accept criticism and direction.

Best Answer: Begin by emphasizing the extremely positive feedback you've gotten throughout your career and that your performance reviews have been uniformly excellent, if that is the case.

No one is perfect, however, and you always welcome suggestions on how to improve your performance. Then, give an example of a not-too damaging learning experience from early in your career and relate the ways this lesson has since helped you.

If you are pressed for a criticism from a recent position, choose something fairly trivial that in no way is essential to your successful performance. Add that you've learned from this, too, and over the past several years or months, it's no longer an area of concern because you now make it a regular practice to do . . .

Question #50: *"Tell me about something you did—or failed to do— that you now feel ashamed of."*

Traps: By now, you probably know you are not going to answer this question. There are some questions your interviewer has no business asking, and this is one of them. While you may feel like answering, "None of your business," naturally you can't. Some interviewers ask this question on the chance you may admit to something, but if not, at least they'll see how you think on your feet.

Best Answer: As with faults and weakness, never confess a regret. But don't seem as if you're stonewalling, either. Say you harbor no regrets, then add a principle or habit you practice regularly for healthy human relations.

Example: Pause for reflection, then say, "You know, I really can't think of anything." Pause again, then add, "As a general management principle, I've found that the best way to avoid regrets is to avoid what causes them in the first place. I practice one habit that helps me a great deal in this regard: At the end of each day, I mentally review the day's events and conversations to take a second look at the people and developments I'm involved with. If I realize I need to correct something in myself or another person, I'll follow up the next day. It could be as simple as giving someone a pat on the back or a five-minute chat in someone's office to make sure that we're clear on things."

Question #51: *The 'Fatal Flaw' Question*

Traps: If an interviewer has read your resume carefully, he may zero in on a "fatal flaw" of your candidacy, perhaps that you don't have a college degree, that you've been out of the job market for some time, that you haven't earned your CPA when most persons in that position have, and so on.

A fatal flaw question can be deadly, but usually only if you respond by being overly defensive.

Best Answer: Whenever you come up against a fatal flaw question, be completely honest, open and straightforward about admitting the shortcoming, since showing you have nothing to hide diminishes the buyer's anxiety.

Do not apologize or try to explain it away. You know that this supposed flaw is nothing to be concerned about, and that this is the attitude you want your interviewer to adopt, as well. Add that as desirable as such a qualification might be, its lack has made you work all the harder throughout your career and has not prevented you from compiling an outstanding record of achievements.

Question #52: *"What's the toughest decision you've ever had to make?"*

Traps: Giving an unprepared or irrelevant answer.

Best Answer: Be prepared with a good example, explaining why the decision was difficult, what process you followed to reach it, how you courageously and effective carried it out, and what the beneficial results were.

Question #53: *"Where could you use some improvement?"*

Traps: This is another tricky way to get you to admit weaknesses. Don't fall for it.

Best Answer: Keep this answer, like all your answers, positive. A good way to answer this question is to identify a cutting-edge branch of your profession—one that's not essential to your employer's needs—as an area you're very excited about and want to explore more fully over the next six months.

Question #54: *"Who has inspired you in life, and why?"*

Traps: The two traps here are unpreparedness and irrelevance. If you grope for an answer, it seems you've never been inspired. If you ramble about your high school basketball coach, you've wasted an opportunity to present qualities of value to the company.

Best Answer: Have a few heroes in mind, from your mental "Board of Directors": leaders in your industry, historical figures, someone who has been your mentor.

Be prepared to give examples of how their words, actions and/or teachings have helped inspire your achievements. As always, prepare an answer which highlights qualities that would be valuable in the position you are seeking. Your interview doesn't really care about your heroes. He cares if you will do a good job.

Question #55: *"What good books have you read recently?"*

Traps: As in all matters of your interview, never fake a familiarity you don't possess. Yet you don't want to seem like a dullard who hasn't read a book since Tom Sawyer in junior high.

Best Answer: It is recommended that you read a handful of the most recent and influential books about your profession and on management.

Consider it a part of your on-going professional development to always be doing some professional reading. But make sure the books you mention in an interview reflect favorably upon you. For example, discussing a best seller which explains how some companies sustained superb growth for over a decade tells the interviewer that you're interested in best business practices. On the other hand, a best seller on how to exit corporate life, work only a few hours a week and pursue your bliss might tell your potential boss that you are not that committed.

Private Questions Which Should Not Have Been Asked

Question #56: On Confidential Matters

Traps: When an interviewer presses you to reveal confidential information about a present or former employer, you may feel it's a no-win situation. If you cooperate, you could be judged as untrustworthy. If you don't cooperate, you may irritate the interviewer and seem obstinate, uncooperative, or overly suspicious.

Best Answer: Don't divulge confidential information.

Your interviewer may press you for this information for two reasons. First, many companies use interviews to research their competition. It's a perfect setup. Here, in their own lair, is an insider from the enemy camp who can reveal prized information on the competition's plans, research, financial condition, etc. Second, the company may be testing your integrity to see if you can be cajoled or bullied into revealing confidential data.

What to do? The answer here is easy. Never reveal anything truly confidential about a present or former employer. By all means, explain your reticence diplomatically. For example, **"I certainly want to be as open as I can about that. But I also wish to respect the rights of those people who've trusted me with their most sensitive information, just as you would hope to be able to trust any of your key people when talking with a competitor."**

Remember that this question pits your desire to be cooperative against your integrity. Faced with any such choice, always choose integrity. It is a far more valuable commodity than whatever information the company can pry from you. Moreover, once you surrender the information, your stock goes down. They will surely lose respect for you.

One company president we know always presses candidates unmercifully for confidential information. If he doesn't get it, he grows visibly annoyed, relentlessly inquisitive. It's all an act. He couldn't care less about the information. This is his way of testing the candidate's moral fiber. Only those candidates who hold fast are hired.

Question #57: "What are your outside interests?"

Traps: You want to be well-rounded, not a drone. But your potential employer will be even more turned off if he suspects that your heavy extracurricular load will interfere with your commitment to your work duties.

Best answer: Try to gauge how this company's culture would look upon your favorite outside activities and answer accordingly.

If you are interviewing at Patagonia, for example, being a surfer, rock climber, kayaker or extreme skier is in your favor. Ditching work when the surf is up is part of their company culture. Yet if you're interviewing for an elementary school teaching position, revealing that you are an aspiring actor and often need to be gone for auditions is not a plus as far as the principal is concerned.

You can also use this question to shatter any stereotypes that could limit your chances. If you're over 50, for example, describe activities that demonstrate physical stamina, like competitive swimming. If you're younger, mention an activity that connotes wisdom and institutional trust, such as serving on the board of a local charity.

But, above all, remember that your employer is hiring you for what you can do for the company and not for your family, yourself or your outside interests, no matter how admirable those activities may be.

Question #58: The Blatant Illegal Question

Traps: Illegal questions include any ones regarding your age, number and ages of your children or other dependents, marital status, maiden name, religion, political affiliation, ancestry, national origin, birthplace, naturalization of your parents, spouse or children, diseases, disabilities, clubs, or your spouse's occupation, unless any of the above are directly related to your performance of the job. You can't even be asked about arrests, though you can be asked about convictions.

Best Answer: Under the ever-present threat of lawsuits, most interviewers are well aware of these taboos. Yet you may encounter, usually on a second or third interview, a senior executive who doesn't interview much and forgets that he can't ask such questions.

You can handle an illegal question in several ways. First, you can assert your legal right not to answer. But this could frighten or embarrass your interviewer and destroy any rapport you had.

Second, you could swallow your concerns over privacy and answer the question straightforwardly if you feel the answer could actually help you. For example, your interviewer, a devout Baptist, recognizes you from church and mentions it.

Third, if you don't want your privacy invaded, you can diplomatically answer the *concern* behind the question without answering the question itself.

Example: If you are 50 and are asked, "How old are you?" you can answer with a friendly, smiling question of your own on whether there's a concern that your age may affect your performance. Further follow up by reassuring the interviewer that there's nothing in this job that you can't do and, in fact, your age and experience are the most important advantages you offer the employer for the reasons you then enumerate.

Another example: If you are a young, married woman and are asked, "Do you plan to have children?" you could again smile, and answer, "My concern right now is to secure a position and wholeheartedly dedicate myself to doing a fantastic job." Then return to how your qualifications mesh with the employer's needs.

Question #59: The 'Secret' Illegal Question

Traps: Much more frequent than the Blatant Illegal Question above is the Secret Illegal Question. It's secret because it's asked only in the interviewer's mind. Since it's not even expressed to you, you have no way to respond to it, and it can, therefore, be most damaging.

Example: You're physically challenged, or a single mother returning to your professional career, or over 50, or a member of an ethnic minority, or you fit any of a dozen other categories that do not strictly conform to the majority of a given company. Most likely, if you are "different" in some way, you're sensitive to it.

Your interviewer wonders, "Is this person really able to handle the job? Is he or she a 'good fit' at a place like ours? Will the chemistry ever be right with someone like this?" But the interviewer never raises such questions because they're illegal. So what can you do?

Best Answer: Remember that just because the interviewer doesn't ask an illegal question doesn't mean he isn't pondering one. More than likely, he's going to come up with his own answer. So you might as well help him out. How? Well, you obviously can't respond to an illegal question he hasn't asked; this may well offend him. And there's always the chance he wasn't even concerned about the issue until you brought it up, and only then begins to wonder.

So, you can't address "secret" illegal questions head-on, but what you can do is make sure there's enough counterbalancing information to more than reassure him that there's no problem in the area he may be doubtful about.

For example, let's say you're a sales rep who had polio as a child and you need a cane to walk. You know your condition has never impeded your performance, yet you're concerned that your interviewer may secretly be wondering about your stamina or ability to travel. Well, make sure that you hit these abilities very hard, leaving no doubt about your capacity to handle them well. For example, you might mention how much you enjoy travelling or how you swim three days a week to keep fit.

Make sure, without in any way seeming defensive about yourself, that you mention strengths, accomplishments, preferences and affiliations that strongly counterbalance any unspoken concerns your interviewer may have.

Question #60: The Opinion Question

Traps: "Opinion questions"—such as your view on abortion, or the presidential election, or any controversial subject—should never be asked. Sometimes they come up during a dinner interview when the interviewer has had a drink or two, is feeling relaxed and is spouting off about something that bugged him in today's news. If you give your opinion and it's the opposite of his, you won't change his opinion, but you could easily lose the job offer.

Best Answer: In these instances, just remember the tale about the student and the wise old rabbi. The scene is a seminary, where an overly serious student is pressing the rabbi to answer the ultimate questions concerning suffering, life and death. But no matter how hard the student presses, the wise old rabbi will only answer each question with a question of his own.

In exasperation, the seminary student demands, "Why, rabbi, do you always answer a question with another question?" To which the rabbi asks, "And why not?"

If you are ever uncomfortable with any question, asking a question in return is the greatest escape hatch ever invented. It throws the onus back on the other person, sidetracks the discussion from going into an area of risk to you, and gives you the time to think of your answer, or even better, your next question!

In response to any of the "opinion" questions cited above, merely responding, "Why do you ask?" will usually dissipate any pressure to give your opinion.

But if your interviewer presses you for an opinion, you can ask another question like, "Is a person's view on gay marriage important when it comes to quality control in manufacturing motherboards?"

Or you could assert a generality with which almost everyone would agree. For example, if your interviewer is complaining about politicians, then suddenly turns to you and asks if you're a Republican or Democrat, you could respond by saying, "Actually, it's hard for me to find any politicians I like these days."

Of course, your best question of all may be whether you want to work for someone so opinionated, but this is one you don't want to ask audibly!

Question #61: _"If you won a $10 million lottery, would you still work?"_

Traps: Your totally honest answer might be, "Hell, no! Are you serious?" That might be so, but any answer which shows you fleeing work if given the chance could make you seem lazy. On the other hand, if you answer, "Oh, I'd want to keep doing exactly what I am doing, only do it for your firm," you could easily inspire your interviewer to silently mutter to himself, "Yeah, sure. Gimme a break."

Best Answer: This type of question is aimed at getting at your bedrock attitude toward work and how you feel about what you currently do. Your best answer will focus on your positive feelings. For example:

- "After I floated down from cloud nine, I think I would still hold to my basic belief that achievement and purposeful work are essential to a happy, productive life. After all, if money alone brought happiness, then all rich people would be happy, and that's not always true."

- "I love the work I do, and I think I'd always want to be involved in my career in some fashion. Winning the lottery would make it more fun because it would mean having more flexibility, more options . . . who knows?"

- "Of course, since I can't count on winning, I'd just as soon create my own destiny by sticking with what's worked for me, meaning good old reliable hard work and a desire to achieve. I think those qualities have built many more fortunes than all the lotteries put together."

Question #62: "Do you consider yourself lucky?"

Traps: This is one of those off-the-wall questions designed to catch you off-guard and provide a glimpse of your self-image or general outlook on life. Also, some bosses actually believe in "luck" and try to surround themselves with lucky people.

In any case, the worst thing you can blurt out is, "Oh, no, I'm not lucky at all. I've never even won a raffle prize."

Best Answer: "Yes, I do consider myself lucky. First, I feel very blessed to have [my good health, spouse, family, etc.] and to live in the greatest country on earth.

"I also feel that I have something of a lucky streak going in my work, primarily because I always try to expect the best. More often than not, you tend to get what you expect—so why not expect the best?

"Above all, I believe in making my own good luck. I live by the saying, 'The harder I work, the luckier I get.'"

Question #63: "Tell me something negative you've heard about our company."

Traps: This is a fishing expedition to see what the industry grapevine might be saying about the company. But it's also a trap because, as an outsider, you never want to be the bearer of unflattering news or gossip about the firm. It can only hurt your chances and sidetrack the interviewer from getting sold on you.

Best Answer: Just remember the rule—never be negative—and you'll handle this one just fine.

Question #64: "On a scale of 1 to 10, rate me as an interviewer."

Traps: Give a perfect "10" and you'll seem too easy to please. Give anything less than a perfect 10, and he could press you as to where you're being critical, and that road leads downhill for you.

Best Answer: Once again, never be negative. The interviewer will only resent criticism coming from you. This is a time to show how positive you are.

Do not, however, give a numerical rating. Simply praise whatever interview style he's been using.

If he's been tough, say, "You have been very thorough and tough-minded, the very qualities most needed to conduct a good interview." If he's been methodical, say, "You have been very methodical and analytical, and I'm sure that approach results in excellent hires for your firm."

In other words, pay him a sincere compliment that he can believe because it's anchored in the behavior you've just seen.

Where Are We Now in The Job Search?

Looking at job-finding business as a three-part process—preparation, engagement with the world, and closing the deal—we have now completed the second phase.

You have sold yourself to the extent of getting an offer or multiple offers. The last step is closing the deal in a way that leaves both you and the hiring party satisfied.

Prudence, otherwise known as sound decision making, is one of the most noble and necessary of all the virtues. It is the habit of good judgment in making practical decisions.

Synonyms for prudence are foresight and wisdom. Prudence is the ability to see what will come of various actions so you can choose the one which will do the most good in a given situation.

The opposite of prudence is negligence or rashness; that is, a failure to think about the consequence of one's actions. Another is what might be called Machiavellian craftiness, when one deviously plans one's actions to get away with evil.

The 64 questions in this chapter will help you develop a great deal of prudence in speech as you practice applying a few key principles to a wide variety of very difficult questions. Some of these principles include:

- Never speak negatively, either in regard to others or yourself; instead be positive.

- Never tell the questioner anything he has no business asking.

- Answer the questions the interviewer **should** be asking.

CHAPTER 9: NEGOTIATING EMPLOYMENT & COMPENSATION

"Any business arrangement that is not profitable to the other person will in the end prove unprofitable for you. The bargain that yields mutual satisfaction is the only one that is apt to be repeated." — B. C. Forbes

In This Chapter:

✓ *Negotiation is a skill you can learn*

✓ *Compare your offer or offers to your ideal job and to each other*

✓ *Know how much you need and how much you are worth*

✓ *Your company will probably either offer you their 'first, best offer' or expect you to negotiate for more than they are offering*

✓ *Everything can be negotiated to make the deal better*

✓ *Shoot for a fair offer that leaves both parties happy to begin your new relationship*

It might seem that your employment negotiation process begins only when a company offers you a job. In reality, it started when you researched general market conditions, typical salary and compensation benchmarks for the job you're seeking, and everything you could find out about the company that ended up making you an offer. On top of that, the process **continued** with all the communications you exchanged with the company who would make the offer.

But now, with an actual offer on the table, explicit negotiations begin in earnest. Don't forget that up until this point you have primarily been selling yourself to the company. Now the people at the company want you and are amenable to selling themselves to you.

After the initial offer, the negotiation process goes through a series of counter-offers and concludes with a mutually agreed-upon employment and compensation package. All of this, of course, assumes a job offer in which negotiation is possible. In many non-management positions, one is simply told what the offer is, and it becomes a take-it-or-leave-it proposition. On the other hand, it may still be possible to play with the package offered: for example, exchanging less of one benefit that does not matter to you for more of another which does.

Decision Time

When it comes to negotiating, you are not going to act based on your feelings. Instead, you'll call on the cold logic necessary to examine whether this is really the right job for you and, if it is, what money and benefits package are appropriate for you.

In Chapter One, you contemplated your ideal job. This is your best chance to compare the job you've been offered with your ideal one. Most probably you've been – or at least you should have been—thinking about this match since your first contact with the company. However, until the offer is actually made, you don't know exactly what you are getting yourself into.

You may, in fact, have to carry out multiple negotiations simultaneously, so it's a good idea to see if one of the offers clearly fails to meet your criteria which will, in turn, lessen the complexity of your decision-making process.

We suggest developing a table that allows you to assess each position utilizing the criteria that you've placed in your ideal job description. You can also use criteria such as:

- Advancement potential
- Benefits
- Commute
- Compensation
- Company values
- Corporate culture
- Industry outlook
- Interest in the position and daily tasks
- Location
- Reputation of the employer
- Work day and environment

You might reorganize these criteria in rank order, starting with the criterion most important to you, and then compare each offer on that basis. The **Comparing Offers** form at the end of this chapter might be helpful to you. It allows you to compare two or more job offers in light of your ideal job using the criteria listed above.

Negotiation Can Be Learned

The more you know about negotiation, the less daunting it will seem for you.

First, the negotiation process takes two parties. The company that makes you an offer has a negotiation philosophy and tactics. So will you. If you understand the company's approach, you're more likely to reach a win-win outcome, that is, one both you and your employer are happy about.

You also need to know what you are worth to the company. You estimate this worth by determining the benchmark compensation level for your position. By benchmark compensation level, we mean the typical range of salary and benefits that someone in your industry, in this particular geographic area, with your knowledge, experience and skills, typically receives.

Another thing you need is patience. You want to let your potential employer make their offer first so you can fashion a counter-offer based on your research and reading of the employer's offer.

Preparing Yourself for the Negotiating Process

There are two numbers you need to know going into the negotiation. The first is your **personal cash requirement**. The second is the **benchmark salary**. Your personal cash requirement is what you need to live on. The benchmark is what someone like you typically gets paid. Remember the example of Carla in Chapter Seven? Carla's problem was that she didn't realize her personal cash requirement was higher than the benchmark salary for a publications marketer in a new, small, non-profit company. There couldn't be a match between what she thought she needed and what the company thought it could pay her.

What is a Benchmark Salary?

A benchmark salary is a salary range. It is based on:

- The position
- The industry
- The supply and demand for the job
- The level of knowledge, skills, and experience the candidate possesses
- The location

Calculate Your Personal Cash Requirement

You probably already have a good idea of your personal financial obligations. The question is whether, and to what extent, these obligations will change with a new position. If you currently can wear jeans, a T-shirt and flip flops to work but you are moving to a position that requires traditional business attire, then you'll have to include the cost of a new wardrobe, as well as dry cleaning costs. Conversely, if gas is $3.50 a gallon and your commute will drop from 100 miles a day to ten, your cash requirements will also go down.

Calculating how much money you need is more complex when relocation is involved. The cost of living may be different and the move may affect your spouse's income. If the cost of living, including housing, is significantly lower in the area to which you will be relocating, an offer of the same salary you are currently receiving could yield a significant net salary increase for you. On the other hand, moving from a lower cost of living area (like Springfield, Illinois) to a higher cost of living area (like Washington, D.C.) requires a significant raise just to break even.

Researching the Benchmark Salary

If you don't know the benchmark salary for the position offered to you, you can take advantage of various online resources to begin your research:

- **Glassdoor.com:** View salary information for any position or industry in any area. You can specify data by company to see what employees earn at over 180,000 companies worldwide. Glassdoor also provides information about benefits including tips and bonuses so you can get the full compensation picture. With data imputed by current and former employees directly, and no way for the employers to pay to have

148

reviews removed, it's a great resource for reliable and transparent information about what it's like to work in a specific firm.

- **Salary.com:** This site is well-respected and will provide both numbers and background information. There are two features that can be of use to you. The Personal Salary Report provides salary information and negotiation tips, while The Job Valuation Report is designed for executives and HR professionals as a summary of all relevant compensation data.

- **Bureau of Labor Statistics:** Find information about industry trends, business costs, occupations, inflation & prices, unemployment, unemployment rates, and regional resources. The Pay & Benefits tab under the Subject drop down can provide insight on local industry wages, work stoppages, compensation cost trends, benefits, and integrated data from numerous BLS National Compensation Surveys.

- **PayScale.com:** Use this site to determine your own with and acquire salary information for your current position, evaluate a job offer, or research a job that is not your own. Staffing managers can also use PayScale to help gauge how much a particular candidate should be offered based on their experience and position.

Remember, you can also use your extended network to learn more about the going rates in a given industry, region, or company.

Do I Need a Lawyer?

Whether you should employ a lawyer depends on the level of the position and the complexity of the compensation package. If your offer straightforward and appears standard for your industry, then you're probably fine on your own.

Senior and "C-Suite" level packages, however, can contain complex salary, bonus, stock, pension, and equity issues which call for experience in evaluating the offer and negotiating a satisfactory deal. Having an attorney review your offer or even negotiate on your behalf can both make you money and give you peace of mind.

Negotiation Strategies

There are two basic strategies companies employ in hiring: "first, best offer" and "low offer with negotiation expected."

Elements in their decision of which approach to take can include:

- The employer's perception of the importance of the work you will be doing
- The supply and demand for persons with your skills and experience in the industry
- The employer's view of how strong your qualifications are for the position
- Your salary history or range
- Their perception of your negotiation skills
- The employer's general philosophy

The strategy that you adopt in response to that of the company will affect your earnings for years to come. At the same time, your best interests are served by accepting a fair offer and not coming across as so difficult (or even greedy) that you create ill will, which is hardly a good way to begin your relationship with your new employer.

"First Offer Is Best Offer" Strategy

With the "first, best offer" strategy, the company analyzes the market and develops one offer. The company hopes to present you a first-and-best deal that you will accept without extensive or derisive negotiation.

If the hiring manager carefully explains the company's philosophy and methodology and presents a detailed review of the market in comparison to your skill and experience level, that's a pretty good indication the company is making a "best offer."

Countering This Strategy:

The problem with this strategy for you is that it is predicated on the company believing it has already done the best for you—and itself—that it can. The company's careful examination of the metrics of the market and its analysis of your skills preclude you from arguing that they are low-balling you. Further, the company's approach is designed to offer what it believes is a win-win situation. Thus, your objections can look unreasonable to the person who wants to hire you.

The strategy that you can employ in this scenario is to first acknowledge the best parts of the offer, such as benefits, bonuses, sign-on, etc. You want to be positive and appreciative. You should also stress the win-win nature of your mindset.

The countering strategies listed below are not in order of importance. Each situation is unique, and you have to match your strategy to your specific situation.

- Suggesting that the offer in its totality does not meet your needs or even current compensation levels.
- Reviewing the offer and placing into play the idea that your job could be expanded and that you can take on more responsibility. You are enhancing the job description which would justify increased compensation.
- Asking for changes to the offer one at a time in a low-key and positive manner

Some non-salary modifications could include:

- Adding a signing bonus or increasing it.
- Changes in any relocation package.
- Increased vacation time.
- Having the company pick up more of your expenses, such as your share of the health insurance.
- Speeding up the review process for the first salary increase, such as having the first review in six months instead of a year.

"Negotiation is Expected" Strategy

In this second strategy, the company or hiring authority philosophy is to make an offer that is below the benchmark salary. The offer could be based on either maintaining or offering only a small increase in your current compensation. This strategy is predicated on establishing a negotiating position. The motives using "negotiation is expected" could range from low-balling you to see if the company can save some money, to wanting to see you negotiate in order to assess your negotiating skills.

Countering This Strategy:

Recognizing this negotiating strategy should be fairly easy. While it may be presented as "our best offer," your thorough research concerning benchmark salaries and the market should alert you that it is, in fact, a low-ball offer. It is imperative that you not react to this offer with emotion— whether incredulity or hostility. Instead, you should point out that:

- You appreciate the offer and that you very much desire to work for the company

- You seek a package that will be a win-win and that will set the tone for a great working relationship with the company
- The offer is below market-value based on your experience and accomplishments
- The offer is even your current compensation package, if this is the case

In developing a counter to the offer, it's good to consider all aspects of the package and determine those aspects that are satisfactory or most easily settled. Just as in sales, you want to get your "customer"—in this case, your future employer—to fall into a pattern of easy and rapid agreement to set the stage for discussing the tough points in the package. So, begin with the ones you both agree on, and then move on to those on which you are very close. If these points are actually minor matters to you, but there is disagreement, don't hesitate to say something like, "Why don't we come back to them later?" In this way, you could use them as concessions you give up in exchange for things you really do want. For example, if a company car doesn't matter to you but family medical coverage does, you can give up the car if they will give in on the medical insurance.

Here are some general strategies you can use to negotiate a better deal:

- Present your view of (1) what the salary norms are for the position and (2) your skills and accomplishments, and, based on that, (3) what you feel is a fair base salary.
- Suggest adding an annual bonus or enhancing the one they have offered as an alternative to a low-starting salary.
- Discuss any changes in relocation package or have it built into the signing bonus.
- Discuss increasing vacation time or the company picking up more of the currently shared costs, for example, of medical insurance.
- Discuss speeding up the review process for the first salary increase, such as having the initial review in six months instead of a year.
- Put into play the idea that your job could be expanded and that you can take on more responsibility. You are enhancing the job description which would justify increased compensation.

The way you handle this negotiation sets the standard for your relationship with the company. The concept of win-win is a matter of perspective, and you should be aware that your perspective may not be the same as that of the company's or its negotiator's.

The numbers you pick for making your counter-offer will vary based on the approach you and the company have taken. When the benchmark salary appears to be the basis of the company's offer, your response must be predicated on factors that would justify placing you higher within that range. Such factors would be your background, education, expertise and achievements, cost of living, high demand for your skills, and so on.

How do you determine the counter offer number? It's a matter of judging the company's willingness to bend and what you feel is acceptable. We think that a five to ten percent above the benchmark might be a good place for you to start.

If you revealed your current salary and other compensation during an interview or on an application, you've made your position more difficult. The company knows your bottom-line and has used it in making its offer. The counter-offer that you fashion must therefore provide a new basis for calculating your salary. For example,

- The responsibilities in the position that you've been offered exceed those of your former position. Thus, the position is worth a salary increase of five percent or more; or

- Increased experience since your last raise dictates that your new salary should be higher.

What do you do if the offer is based on the company's own salary range? Employers often have an established salary range for the position being offered. The employer through HR or the hiring manager then determines what percentage of the range you will be offered. Many employers will offer experienced candidates from 50 to 70 percent of the range.

The argument you make for an increased percentage of that range has to be an appeal to the level of your expertise and, therefore, your value to the company. It may also be helpful to point out or propose enhanced responsibilities that are normally not undertaken by individuals in that position. Expanded responsibilities can justify increasing the percentage of—or even upgrading—the salary range.

When you feel the offer is too low, you can say...

"I like the job and I think my skills would be an asset to your team. I would be willing to start in two weeks. However, I cannot justify doing that with the initial salary offer. How much room do we have for negotiation?"

or

"I could definitely start on [date]. My background and experience would work well with the goals you have for the job. The only thing standing in the way of my saying yes is the initial salary offer. I am extremely interested in the job and excited that you see me working with you. If we could solve this money issue, I'm sure we could negotiate a package. What can we do?"

Other Issues That Can Be Negotiated

Potentially, every element of compensation can be negotiated and we have included what we believe is a comprehensive list. Since we want to be thorough, we have included all the following elements. That stated, exercise prudence in bringing them up.

AIR TRAVEL
- First-class, limited or unlimited
- Airline VIP lounge memberships

AUTOMOBILE/PARKING
- Company car
- Auto allowance
- Reimbursement for use of personal car for business
- Paid parking

BONUS STRUCTURES
- Signing
- Annual
- Criteria for bonus

COMPANY-PAID RELOCATION
- Moving costs
- Travel or hotel costs for employee and family
- Mortgage assistance, brokerage fees, etc.

DEFERRED COMPENSATION
- Stock options
- 401(k)
- Tax-deferred annuity plan

EDUCATION ASSISTANCE PROGRAMS
- Percentage of actual costs reimbursed
- Maximum per year
- Work-related or other limitations

EMPLOYEE ASSISTANCE PROGRAMS
- Counseling for employee
- Counseling for family
- Substance abuse, etc.

EXECUTIVE-ONLY FACILITIES
- Country club: Golf, tennis, health or athletic clubs
- Luncheon clubs
- Company-operated clubs or gym facilities

GENERAL
- Job descriptions – or at least some of its details
- Starting date
- Starting bonus
- Title
- Decision-making authority including support staff, budget and resources
- Reporting Relationship

INSURANCE (Life, Disability, Accident, Travel, Liability)
- Size and scope of benefits
- Percentage of monthly premium paid by company
- Travel insurance
- Personal liability arising from execution of job duties, such as product liability

MEDICAL PLAN
- Type of plan (Indemnity, PPO, HMO)
- Choice of care providers
- Percentage of monthly premium paid by company
- Co-Payment and deductible
- Percentage reimbursement
- Mental healthcare
- Vision plan
- Dental plan

PAID HOLIDAYS
- Number per year
- Flexibility of usage
- Personal days
- Compensation for unused days
- Carry-over or accrual provisions

PROFESSIONAL/TRADE ASSOCIATION MEMBERSHIP & DUES
- Certification or license cost reimbursement
- Costs of participation in association meetings or programs

RETIREMENT PENSION PLAN
- Type of plan
- Vesting schedule

SICK LEAVE
- Number of days per year
- Flexibility of usage
- Compensation for unused days
- Carry-over or accrual provisions

VACATION
- Number of days first year
- Schedule for subsequent years
- Compensation for unused days
- Supplemental vacation

General Negotiating Guidelines and Tips

While each negotiation is going to be different, the following are some general strategies and tips that might be helpful.

Tone and Tenor

- Show enthusiasm about everything: the job, the future boss and the opportunity. Stay positive.

- Keep your discussions on an impersonal level, and be as businesslike and logical as you can. Do not try to do all the negotiations in one session if the issues are complex or if things become contentious. This prudent approach also allows you to seek advice between conversations.

<u>Evaluation of Offers</u>

- Evaluate all offers. Never accept or reject an offer in the moment. Even if you are sure you will say yes, wait a day.

- Evaluate offers based on your ideal job.

- Seek advice from mentors or advisors—but remember that you're responsible for your own decisions.

- Don't ignore or underrate the total compensation package. Salary is important and crucial, but other considerations matter too. For example, fully paid family medical insurance could add 5,000 net salary dollars or more to your bottom line.

<u>Salary Negotiation</u>

Don't reveal your salary requirements in the interview process. You may lose your leverage for future negotiations.

- Don't exaggerate your present income. It is very easy for an organization to verify any figure that you give them. Some companies even ask for your W-2 forms or your last three pay stubs.

- As discussed earlier, you can play around with the difference between the salary the company pays you and total cost of your package to them. For example, your current salary could be $75,000, but the total cost to your employer once all benefits and taxes are taken into account could be $110,000. So you could say, "My current package is worth $110,000; I'd be willing to start for an annual salary of $85,000."

- If you cannot get one thing, try for something else. If the company is adamant about salary, try for a guaranteed bonus, a performance incentive, or added benefits.

- Include in your thinking all compensation such as bonuses, profit sharing, equity issues, tangible non-cash compensation such as company car or club memberships, as well as benefits like medical and disability policies. Everything that you need and would willingly pay for yourself is like income for you if you can get the employer to pay for it. For example, if you are carrying a $250,000-term life insurance policy that costs $1000 a year and your employer offers to give you a policy equal to the one you have, you have just saved $1000.

- If you don't meet with any success in your negotiation concerning the present, concentrate on the future, such as review in six months or an automatic increase after 12 months.

The Silent Treatment

The Silent Treatment is a tactic used by some companies to see how you respond under pressure and possibly derail negotiations through means of discomfort. Here's an example of how it works:

> Your potential employer makes an offer to you about your salary or benefits that does not fall within your benchmark salary range.

> You then ask a question or provide a counter-offer only for them to stare at you in a deafening silence instead of honoring your counter with a response.

> You wait, growing a bit uneasy, and there they sit, silent as a face on Mt. Rushmore, as if they don't believe what you've just said, or perhaps they're making you feel that you've unwittingly violated some cardinal rule of negotiating etiquette.

In an effort to end the prolonged, uncomfortable silence, an unprepared candidate might rush in to expand on their reasoning or explain their needs further and potentially clarify any issues that may have caused some problem.

Although the reaction to fill void is well-intentioned, this is exactly the **opposite** of what you **should** be doing! A candidate who rambles on, sputtering more and more information, is more likely to talk themselves **out** of their own firm stance and actually start agreeing with the offer made by the other side.

Whatever you do, don't let the Silent Treatment intimidate you into talking a blue streak, because you could easily jabber yourself out of the position. Like the primitive tribal mask, the Silent Treatment loses all its power to frighten you once you refuse to be intimidated. If you find yourself in a similar situation, keep quiet for a while and then ask, with sincere politeness and not a trace of sarcasm, "Is there anything else I can fill in on that point?"

<u>Closing the Deal</u>

Now that you are close to having made your job search campaign a successful one, it is very important that you do not do anything that might compromise your chances. This isn't the time to take foolish risks or to stop doing your homework. Too many sure things have been known to slip away at the last minute simply because they were taken for granted.

Some final words of caution:

- Agree on a decision date and be sure to give your answer by then.

- Unless you have a contract, don't cut off other options until you have actually started work. Until you're on the payroll, you don't have anything more than the employer's word.

- If possible, try to get the employer to put the deal in writing. A letter confirming employment and terms is the most common form. If the company seems reluctant, write the letter yourself, asking them to agree to your understanding of the terms.

- Be certain that no contingencies remain up in the air. For example, have all reference and security checks been made? Have you passed the physical if one is required?

- Don't spread the word about your employment until you are truly on board. Keep it within your circle of close associates until it is finalized.

- Once you've started your new job, remember to contact all the people who helped you in your job search. Thank them for their time and interest in you. You never can tell when you might need their assistance again, and you want them to remain a permanent part of your network.

Gratitude. One of the characteristics of human excellence any decent person should cultivate is gratitude. Gratitude is thankfulness for the goods that one has received. Gratitude is shown both in counting your blessings and in actually saying thank you to the persons who have helped you.

If you think about it, many people have helped you find your new position. You should thank them explicitly. You can also "pay them back" by helping them when the occasion arises.

Gratitude should be a virtue or habit. Therefore, it is not supposed to be a one-time outpouring of emotion based on an instance of good fortune which quickly passes and begins to be taken for granted.

We recommend that you spend a few minutes each day, every day, counting your blessings. Each one of us is blessed in many ways: We would be blind and ungrateful if we didn't acknowledge this truth. This "attitude of gratitude" also corresponds with reality and will help us be happier people.

An overflowing of the virtue of gratitude can be seen in helping people who have done nothing for you. You can accomplish such feats by becoming a mentor and offering sincere service to everyone with whom you come in contact.

THE COMPARING OFFERS FORM

CRITERIA	IDEAL JOB	OFFER A	OFFER B
Benefits			
Commute			
Compensation			
Company Values			
Corporate Culture			
Daily Tasks			
Employer's Reputation			
Industry Outlook			
Interest in Position			
Location			
Work Day			
Work Environment			

FINAL WORDS

Now that you have your dream position, commit yourself to finding your next job. By this, we don't mean start **looking** for a new job, sending out resumes, and so on. What we mean is, start doing the best thing you can do to always be employed: network. Stay in touch with the people you know. Constantly expand your circle. Mentor folks who are not as far along in their careers as you are. Seek out mentors who can help you. Above all, look for opportunities to perform sincere service to those individuals with whom you network.

APPENDIX A: RESUME ACTION WORDS

Analytical/Financial

Accounted for	Monitored	Revived
Administered	Multiplied	Satisfied
Allocated	Planned	Scrutinized
Analyzed	Procured	Secured
Appraised	Projected	Sought
Audited	Provided	Settled
Balanced	Purchased	Staffed
Budgeted	Raised	Strengthened
Calculated	Rated	Submitted
Controlled	Reconciled	Substantiated
Developed	Refined	Suggested
Estimated	Reformed	Supplemented
Financed	Regarded	Sustained
Forecasted	Related	Supplemented
Managed	Relieved	Sustained
Marketed	Remedied	Tailored
Minimized	Researched	Transferred
Mobilized	Reserved	

Communication

Addressed	Edited	Networked
Arbitrated	Formulated	Persuaded
Arranged	Influenced	Presented
Authored	Informed	Promoted
Communicated	Interpreted	Publicized
Composed	Interviewed	Published
Contacted	Lectured	Reconciled
Convinced	Marketed	Recruited
Corresponded	Mediated	Referred
Developed	Moderated	Reported
Directed	Motivated	Translated
Drafted	Negotiated	Wrote

Communication

Acted	Founded	Remodeled
Composed	Improvised	Renovated
Conceived	Instituted	Replaced
Conceptualized	Integrated	Revitalized
Conducted	Introduced	Shaped
Created	Invented	Sketched
Designed	Marketed	Spearheaded
Developed	Modernized	Started
Directed	Originated	Stimulated
Drafted	Performed	Strategized
Established	Pioneered	Transformed
Executed	Planned	
Fashioned	Redesigned	

Drive/ Results

Accelerated	Established	Proved
Accomplished	Exceeded	Reduced
Achieved	Expanded	Re-established
Attained	Improved	Resolved
Augmented	Increased	Restored
Completed	Initiated	Selected as
Compounded	Introduced	Stabilized
Contributed	Launched	Standardized
Decreased	Lowered costs	Succeeded
Doubled	Maximized	Transformed
Effected	Measured	Trimmed
Eliminated	Obtained	Validated
Enlarged	Pioneered	

Ideas/Data

Adapted	Initiated	Presented
Analyzed	Integrated	Processed
Coordinated	Maintained	Proposed
Defined	Manipulated	Publicized
Devised	Marketed	Recommended
Established	Modified	Recorded
Executed	Monitored	Related
Explained	Negotiated	Surveyed
Illustrated	Obtained	Translated
Implemented	Persuaded	Wrote

Management/Leadership

Accounted for	Correlated	Managed
Administered	Cultivated	Organized
Analyzed	Delegated	Oversaw
Centralized	Determined	Planned
Certified	Developed	Prioritized
Chaired	Employed	Produced
Changed	Evaluated	Proposed
Commissioned	Executed	Recommended
Committed	Formulated	Recruited
Concluded	Founded	Regulated
Condensed	Fulfilled	Reviewed
Confirmed	Grew	Revitalized
Consented	Handled	Set goals
Consolidated	Headed	Scheduled
Contracted	Hired	Supervised
Consulted	Maintained	

Organizational/Time Management

Approved	Generated	Retrieved
Arranged	Identified	Revamped
Cataloged	Implemented	Revised
Classified	Inspected	Scheduled
Collaborated	Integrated	Screened
Collected	Monitored	Shaped
Compiled	Operated	Specialized
Conserved	Organized	Specified
Consolidated	Prepared	Streamlined
Distributed	Prioritized	Systematized
Enlisted	Processed	Tabulated
Executed	Recorded	Targeted
Expedited	Reorganized	Updated
Extracted	Reshaped	Validated

People

Accomplished	Chaired	Distributed
Activated	Collaborated	Directed
Administered	Conceptualized	Explained
Advertised	Conciliated	Indoctrinated
Advised	Conducted	Managed
Analyzed	Consulted	Organized
Arranged	Contracted	Programmed
Assembled	Coordinated	Promoted
Assisted	Delegated	Supervised
Calculated	Demonstrated	
Catalogued	Devised	

Quantitative/Research

Acquired	Examined	Judged
Amplified	Extracted	Justified
Analyzed	Formulated	Led
Approximated	Grew	Licensed
Ascertained	Guaranteed	Linked
Attested	Identified	Minimized
Authorized	Indexed	Modified
Bolstered	Inferred	Organized
Boosted	Innovated	Processed
Calculated	Inspected	Researched
Charted	Inspired	Reviewed
Collected	Instituted	Studied
Compared	Interested	Summarized
Conducted	Interpreted	Surveyed
Diagnosed	Interviewed	Systematized
Designed	Investigated	Tested
Determined	Involved	Trouble-shot
Evaluated	Issued	

Teaching/Helping

Adapted	Clarified	Developed
Advised	Coached	Directed
Analyzed	Communicated	Educated
Applied	Cooperated	Elaborated
Appraised	Corrected	Elicited
Assessed	Defined	Enabled
Assigned	Demonstrated	Evaluated
Categorized	Designed	Explained

Facilitated	Interacted	Rewarded
Generated	Investigated	Simplified
Guided	Modeled	Solicited
Identified	Modified	Speculated
Implemented	Motivated	Stated
Incorporated	Observed	Structured
Indicated	Organized	Synthesized
Informed	Postulated	Systematized
Initiated	Praised	Taught
Instructed	Questioned	Trained
Integrated	Reinforced	Tutored

Technical

Activated	Dispersed	Navigated
Assembled	Displayed	Operated
Built	Elevated	Overhauled
Calculated	Endorsed	Participated
Computed	Enforced	Programmed
Constructed	Engineered	Rehabilitated
Converted	Enhanced	Remodeled
Customized	Enriched	Repaired
Debugged	Excelled	Resolved
Deciphered	Exercised	Retrieved
Dedicated	Exhibited	Screened
Deliberated	Fabricated	Sold
Delivered	Familiarized	Serviced
Designed	Finalized	Solved
Detected	Formed	Supplied
Devaluated	Installed	Trained
Devised	Maintained	Upgraded

The IDEAL JOB Form

ORGANIZATION
In what business or industry would you prefer to work?

_____

_____

_____

RESPONSIBILITIES
Describe your ideal scope of responsibility:

_____

_____

_____

COMPANY CULTURE
Describe the values and ethics of an organization you'd enjoy:

_____

_____

_____

MANAGEMENT STYLE
List daily business approaches you'd like a new employer to possess:

_____

_____

_____

COMPENSATION
What would be your preferred job package and salary?

_____

_____

DAY-TO-DAY
Describe a typical day at your ideal job:

_____

_____

_____

The **TRANSFERRABLE SKILLS** Form

When you have completed this form, review your skills and consider how they may be used in other fields, careers, or industries that interest you.

ANALYTICAL SKILLS: Working with DATA & INFORMATION
Includes evaluation and manipulation of data and information such as budgets, planning, organization, solutions, and providing interpretations.

_____

_____

_____

_____

CONCEPTUAL SKILLS: Working with IDEA
Includes researching, creating, describing, developing, and implementing projects, systems, and procedures.

_____

_____

_____

_____

PEOPLE SKILLS: Working with PEOPLE
Includes management, training, mentoring, coaching, and team-related activities.

_____

_____

_____

_____

SPECIAL SKILLS
Includes unique and specialized abilities (i.e., artistic or financial skills), political acumen within organizations, PR skills, etc.

_____

_____

_____

_____

SAMPLE RESUME

BOB SMITH, CIA

Chicago, IL ● (123) 456-7890 ● YourName@gmail.com ● www.linkedin.com/in/sample123

Certified Internal Auditor with over 15 years of experience in financial, operational and compliance auditing in the healthcare industry. Excellent oral and written communication skills resulting in obtaining financial recoveries and implementing procedural changes. Interfaces effectively with all levels of management.

Career Achievements

123 HEALTH Co. — Los Angeles, CA   2004 – Present
Disbursement Auditor (2011 - Present)
Performed financial and compliance audits of disbursement systems. Reviewed regional procurement and travel cards to ensure compliance with policies and procedures. Performed contract reviews of material and supply vendors, resulting in reimbursement for pricing discrepancies.

- Discovered $370K in overpayments through the review of cost plus contracts.
- Recovered $30K in overcharges due to external vendors not passing along cost savings. Contract terminology was added to all purchasing contracts to ensure the ability to perform audits and recover possible overcharges.

Internal Auditor (2004 - 2011)
Responsible for planning and performing financial, compliance and operational audits. Performed all phases of audit process from the preliminary review through the final report.

- Responsibilities also included the supervision of other auditors and the coordination of findings to all levels of management.
- Performed a review of the regional dues revenue system. Identified $364K in delinquent dues, which were subsequently recovered. Recommended procedures to verify correctness of dues payments.

LA COUNTY CONTROLLER'S OFFICE — Los Angeles, CA   2001 – 2004
Staff Internal Auditor
Supervised and performed operational and financial audits at four different Los Angeles County hospitals. Identified and developed audit areas, developed and wrote audit programs, trained new audit staff and drafted reports to hospital management.

- Assisted in the development of a new billing system for Rancho Vallarta Hospital. Reduced the number of days outstanding in accounts receivable.
- Conducted a contract review of a private hospital, which provides care for Los Angeles County patients. Audit findings disclosed overpayments of $20K.

Education & Training

Bachelor of Science – Business Administration
Pepperdine University, Malibu, CA
Rich Edmund Course Graduate

Affiliations

Member, Institute of Internal Audits
Member, Association of Healthcare Internal Auditors

The **RESUME DEVELOPMENT** Form

THE "WHO I AM" STATEMENT

The "Who I Am" statement consists of two or three sentences:
(1) A description of yourself which contains—a descriptive title or phrase; years of experience; and type of company and industry or industry-sector.
(2) A statement of your major strengths and expertise. And, if warranted,
(3) a second statement of exceptional skills or major strengths.

_____

_____

_____

_____

CAREER ACCOMPLISHMENTS

Starting with the most recent job, complete the following section for each position held in the past 10 to 15 years.

Employer: _____

City, State: _____ From/To: _____

Title: _____

Brief description of responsibilities:

_____

_____

_____

List 3 to 4 achievements (quantifiable, if possible):

- _____

_____

- _____

_____

- _____

_____

EDUCATION (Complete for each degree held)

    Degree: _____

    College/University: _____

    City, State: _____

PROFESSIONAL LICENSURE & CERTIFICATIONS

    Professional License: _____

    License or Certification: _____

TRAINING/SEMINARS

_____

_____

_____

PROFESSIONAL ASSOCIATIONS

_____

_____

_____

The LIFETIME ACHIEVEMENTS-MEMORY JOGGER Form

Examples of achievements are listed below. Work through the following categories and circle any item that applies to you. adding any experience you may have had that is not on the list. Do not include personal interests, salary history, religion, or comments about health or references.

ACADEMIC RECOGNITION

- Dean's List
- Graduation Recognition (i.e., Cum Laude)
- Unique Scholarships/Grants
- Fellowships (i.e., Rhodes, Scholar)
- Other: _____

WORK-RELATED ACCOMPLISHMENTS

- Customer Service Excellence Award
- Awards for making Significant Suggestions
- Appointments to Special or Select Committees or Teams
- Awards for System Creation/Development and Implementation
- Awards for Creating and/or Developing Procedures
- Awards for Cost Savings
- Other: _____

PUBLIC SERVICE AWARDS/NATIONAL RECOGNITION

- Service or Award for National/State/Major City Commission
- Participation/Winner/Nominee in a major award program such as industry awards, arts and performance awards
- Appointment or winning placement on National Team
- Founded non-profit/association/club
- Other: _____

MISCELLANEOUS

- _____
- _____
- _____

Sample "Mirror" Cover Letters

Growing Los Angeles Software company seeks CFO with 10-15 years of experience. Experience with middle market a must. Corporate management background essential. CPA required. Software company experience a big plus. Salary 100K plus bonus and stock options.

The following is a cover letter sent in response to the advertisement above. Here, John Citizen can address his email to a specific person since it was listed in the job posting.

Re: **Chief Financial Officer—Wall Street Journal Posting**

Dear Mr. Smith,

I have been a financial executive for the past 16 years, the last eight with a $90MM maker of computer hard drives. My strengths include developing innovative ways to make financial data accessible to front- line managers for use in daily decisions.

Further qualifications which provide a good match for your advertised position include:

- Extensive middle market company experience.
- Experience as a Controller for a Silicon Valley software developer serving the engineering marketplace.
- CPA from New York University, graduating cum laude.

I appreciate the opportunity to speak with you about the position and I look forward to hearing from you soon.

Sincerely,

John Citizen

Five years proven experience in store management with the ability to train people and to provide leadership in expanding the organization.

Re: **Pet Store Manager—Indeed**

Dear Sir or Madam:

I have been a pet store manager for over 10 years with a track record of increasing sales in excess of inflation for every year since my arrival.

My experience includes:

- Hiring, training and supervising a staff of up to 10 individuals, with a retention rate that averages over three years per employee.
- Increasing profitability of the operation for the last six years.

- Leading opening team for four of the chain's 10 retail stores, providing manager training, hiring assistance, training in marketing and grand-opening advertising campaigns.

Attached is my resume, which highlights my employment history and achievements. I look forward to hearing from you and appreciate your consideration.

Sincerely,

A leader with a proven track record and the ability to train and to provide input and leadership in developing new products to meet market needs.

Re: **Regional Sales Manager—LinkedIn Jobs**

Dear Sir or Madam:

I am a Regional Sales Manager for a major consumer productions manufacturer with over eight years' experience, increasing sales from $2.5MM to $35MM during that time.

My successes include:

- Conceived, developed and implemented a regional sales and expense containment plan that resulted in the highest ROI and profitability for any region. The entire corporation has adopted this plan.
- Managed and directed the efforts of a 12-member sales force with an average sales increase of over 10% per salesperson over the last three years.
- Provided the initial input and led efforts to develop a unique new PDA system that returned the largest first-year ROI of any new product in the company's history.

I appreciate your consideration and look forward to hearing from you soon.

Sincerely,

Sample Generic Cover Letters

Re: **Marketing Director position**

Dear Mr. Jones,

I am a consumer products Marketing Director with over 10 years' experience in the entertainment industry. Expertise and accomplishments include:

- Developing the marketing strategy which increased product impressions by 175%.
- Identifying, negotiating and implementing cooperative cross-marketing agreements which resulted in a 100% increase in cooperative advertising, worth over $2MM in advertising exposure.
- Creating marketing teams which learned from the sales force and clients, resulting in a new product yielding over $1MM in sales in its first year of production.

Enclosed is my resume. I would appreciate an opportunity to discuss my qualifications with you regarding this position. Thank you for your consideration.

Cordially,

The following example highlights job functions in lieu of achievements:

Re: **VP for Information Technology position**

Dear Sir or Madam:

I am a decisive and results-oriented Information Technology Executive. I have over 15 years of experience optimizing an organization's information technology environment through cogent analysis and efficient deployment of cost-effective, reliable and secure architecture, business processes and training.

Expertise includes:

- Input in developing strategic business plans and directing the alignment of the IT strategy's architecture and organization to meet immediate and long-term plan goals.
- Optimization of current hardware and software asset utilization through business process modification and/or prudent capital investment.
- Leadership in a difficult business environment, such as in pre/post-acquisition, corporate leadership change, adverse market conditions or new financial constraints.

Enclosed is my resume for your review. I would appreciate an opportunity to discuss my qualifications with you. Thank you for your consideration.

Sincerely,

Sample "Big Gun" Cover Letter

Notice how much more powerful John Citizen's "big gun" cover letter compares to the "mirror" cover letter he wrote for the same position:

Re: **Chief Financial Officer—Wall Street Journal Posting**

Dear Mr. Smith,

In my last eight years as a stock broker, my annual gross production has never been less than $800K and is usually closer to my high of $1.25MM, reached in the banner year of 2005.

But even in this "leaner and meaner" era on Wall Street, I have turned in a superb performance, averaging about $1MM in gross commission production.

Part of the reason I have been a top producer for the firm is that I have given my clients a highly personal and caring level of service that has kept them fiercely loyal to me.

I would welcome the opportunity to share with you the strategies I have found so successful in this investment marketplace, strategies which have been directly responsible for my being the number one producer in my office for the last four years running.

I will call on Thursday morning to see if you have an interest in setting up an interview. In the meantime, if you have any questions, I may be reached at (444) 555-6666.

Sincerely,

John Citizen

The WRITING YOUR 30-SECOND SUMMARY Form

WHY THIS?
Given what you want to accomplish with your networking, what is your relevant background and experience?

_____

_____

_____

_____

STRENGTHS
Next, list three or four key strengths which you want to include.

1. _____

_____

_____

2. _____

_____

_____

3. _____

_____

_____

4. _____

_____

_____

SUMMARY
Now incorporate the points which you've listed above into the first draft of your summary. Be sure to keep it brief; it should be 30 seconds or less when read.

_____

_____

_____

_____

_____

_____

Practice it out loud. Record it, listen to It, and critique it. Try it out on friends. Revise it. Program it into your memory. Modify it for particular circumstances.

The NETWORKING LIST Form

NAME	TITLE & COMPANY	PHONE	DATE CONTACTED	REFERRED BY

The PLANNING NETWORKING PHONE CALLS/MEETINGS Form
Before the Meeting

PRE-MEETING INFORMATION

Name of Contact: _____

Company: _____

Phone Number/Location: _____

Who Referred: _____

Objectives of Call: 1._____

2._____

3._____

CONVERSATION CONTENT

What will I say to start the conversation?

_____
_____
_____
_____
_____
_____

What are my ideas on how to best approach the contact?

_____
_____
_____
_____
_____

What are my expectations from this meeting?

_____
_____
_____
_____
_____

The PLANNING NETWORKING PHONE CALLS/MEETINGS Form
After the Meeting

POST-MEETING RESULTS

Resume Requested? Y / N   If yes, give to whom?_____

Follow up info (email/phone): _____

Date of Follow-up: _____

Contact Quality:_____

Referrals Provided: 1. _____

2. _____

3. _____

CONVERSATION OVERVIEW

Topics Discussed:

_____

_____

_____

What information can I give them (on me to further conversations, to help them, etc.)?

_____

_____

_____

How can this contact help?

_____

_____

_____

What kind of resource will this person be to me?

_____

_____

_____

Next Steps:

_____

_____

_____

The PRE-INTERVIEW PLANNING Form

INITIAL CONTACT

Date of Initial Contact: _____

Initial Contact Type (LinkedIn, networking event): _____

Company: _____

City/State: _____

Phone: _____

Email: _____

Position: _____

Company's Main Product/ Service: _____

Company Contact Name/Title: _____

Additional Contact(s): _____

INTERVIEW DETAILS

Interview Address: _____

Date: _____

Interviewer Name: _____

Interviewer Contact Info: _____

Additional Interviewer(s): _____

If at a hotel/restaurant, reservation is under what name: _____

What is the interviewer's role? (direct report, recruiter): _____

If hired, who would you report to? _____

INTERVIEW STRATEGY

How are you relevant for the position? _____

_____

_____

_____

Describe relevant accomplishments: _____

_____

_____

_____

_____

Additional points: _____

_____

_____

_____

The POST-INTERVIEW REVIEW Form

Immediately after the interview, write down everything you can remember about the following details.

INTERVIEW DETAILS

Company: _____

Interview Address: _____

Date: _____

Interviewer Name: _____

Interviewer Contact Info: _____

Additional Interviewer(s): _____

If at a hotel/restaurant, reservation is under what name? _____

What is the interviewer's role? (direct report, recruiter): _____

If hired, who would you report to?: _____

INTERVIEW NOTES

The Position—Special Duties/Responsibilities:_____
_____
_____

The Position—Priorities:_____
_____
_____
_____

The Person—What is the Interviewer looking for? _____
_____
_____
_____

The Company—Goals/Outlook/Philosophy:_____
_____
_____
_____

Cast of Characters—Who Were They? Your Reactions To Them?
_____
_____
_____

APPENDIX **B**: Handouts & Forms

The Material (Answers)—What did you tell them? _____

_____

_____

_____

What did you leave out? _____

_____

_____

Information/Clues You Picked Up:_____

_____

_____

Did the interviewer dwell on any one subject or ask a question more than once?

_____

_____

_____

Next Steps:_____

_____

_____

_____

Additional information you'd like to give the interviewer (via email, phone, or follow-up interview):_____

_____

_____

PERFORMANCE NOTES

Your Strengths:_____

_____

_____

_____

Your Weaknesses: :_____

_____

_____

_____

Sample Follow-Up Letter

In this example, the writer has picked up the importance of "Family Atmosphere" which Mr. Cisco mentioned several times during the interview.

Dear Mr. Cisco,

I enjoyed meeting with you yesterday and having the opportunity to learn more about The Cisco Company and your future business plans. I believe we are in agreement that my technical abilities meet with your requirement for the position of Director of Information Services.

What is of equal importance to me is your desire to maintain a family atmosphere within the company. This style of interpersonal relationships is precisely what I have been seeking.

Please consider me an enthusiastic candidate for the position. If you need additional information or clarification, please contact me at (999) 444-5555 or JECitizen@gmail.com.

Sincerely,

Judith E. Citizen.

The **COMPARING OFFERS** Form

CRITERIA	IDEAL JOB	OFFER A	OFFER B
Benefits			
Commute			
Compensation			
Company Values			
Corporate Culture			
Daily Tasks			
Employer's Reputation			
Industry Outlook			
Interest in Position			
Location			
Work Day			
Work Environment			

ABOUT THE FIRM

Hand & Associates is an internationally recognized executive management consulting firm with a primary emphasis on coaching and career transition services. We also offer a variety of management programs that directly address client leadership, placement and training needs.

Founded by J. Kevin Hand in 1991, the company's clients include the medical, biotechnical, petroleum, entertainment and media, insurance and retail industries, as well as colleges and universities.

Our domestically based clients include Target, the Nestle Brand Food Corp, Northrop Grumman, HealthNet, the Federal Reserve Bank, the Cedars-Sinai Health System, Pepperdine University, Federated Department Stores, Fox Animation, Fox Cable, News Corp., Paramount, MGM/UA, MTV Networks, Nickelodeon and NBC Universal.

Some of our international clients have included Corte Ingles (one of Spain's largest retailers), Bertelsmann M.G. (Germany) and Thomson S.A. (France).

By focusing on the individual, Hand & Associates' coaches identify specific needs and create unique programs to address those same needs. In an environment of constant change, Hand & Associates has developed a positive reputation for the array and quality of services provided, resulting in impressive placement and return-business rates.

www.ingramcontent.com/pod-product-compliance
Lightning Source LLC
Chambersburg PA
CBHW030938180526
45163CB00002B/610